MW00398614

PRAISE FOR *LEADING JESUS' WAY*

"There's no doubt in my mind that Jesus was the greatest leadership role model of all time. If you want to find out how he did it—and how you, too, can be a servant leader in your organization—read *Leading Jesus' Way*. I guarantee you will get both great results and great human satisfaction."

—Ken Blanchard, coauthor of
The New One Minute Manager® and *Lead Like Jesus Revisited*

"Mark is a *credible* witness of Jesus-based servant leadership. He speaks it clearly and lives it consistently. *Leading Jesus' Way* is powerful for the same two reasons: Mark gives a clear and grounded case for why leading like Jesus is both good faith and good business, and he speaks with a voice that believes what he says and puts that conviction into practice."

—Rev. Dr. Mark Herringshaw
Partner, GiANT Worldwide

"Servant leadership is a proven path to engaged, productive, caring team members. The idea of servant leadership is well known. What is not well known is HOW to embrace it. *Leading Jesus' Way*, is a proven road map to embracing servant leadership actions every day. The book "clears the path" to creating a purpose driven, values aligned workplace."

—S. Chris Edmonds
Author of the Amazon best seller *The Culture Engine*
DrivingResultsThroughCulture.com

"Leading Jesus' Way will impact leaders of all levels. It combines world-class business teaching with solid Biblical teaching. This is a great 1-2 punch that will absolutely transform your business and personal life. I learned and implemented many concrete action items that are having a positive impact on my business and my life."

—Curt Tillotson
Chief Operating Officer, Nahan Printing, Inc.

"Leading Jesus' Way: Become the Servant Leader God Created You to Be is a gift to leaders who understand that servant-led organizations consistently outperform their peers, but don't know how to become a servant leader themselves and/or build a culture around it. Mark Deterding debunks the myths of servant leadership (no, it's not soft), and gives his readers five practical and proven concepts that will **build** and transform them and the organizations they serve."

—Jon Ballou
President & CEO, Douglas Machine Inc.

"Biblical principles work – the school of hard knocks has reinforced this for me! Aagard has leveraged the servant leadership training that Mark outlines in *Leading Jesus' Way* to build a company that has more fun, wins more often, and better serves its customers."

—Brenton L. Smith
CEO, Aagard Group

"Mark Deterding is a living example of servant leadership, and he has written his book with the same wisdom, dedication and respect that guides his life. Mark shows how servant leadership is not a technique, but an approach that can guide every decision you make as a leader and in all aspects of your life."

—Jesse Lyn Stoner
Coauthor of Full Steam Ahead! Unleash the Power of Vision
and *Leading at a Higher Level*

"Jesus is history's greatest role model of servant leadership. Anyone desiring to be a successful leader would be wise to follow in his footsteps. Mark leads Jesus' way and has dedicated his life and career to helping others unlock their servant leadership potential. You'll find this book provides a clear roadmap to becoming a servant leader and it will become a trusted companion that you'll refer to time and again."

—Randy Conley
V.P. Client Services & Trust Practice Leader,
The Ken Blanchard Companies
Author of the award-winning LeadingWithTrust.com blog.

"Mark Deterding has had a huge impact on my life. I've come to know Mark as a man who not only understands the heart and soul of servant leadership, but also one who truly walks these principles out in his daily life. The principles he shares in *Leading Jesus' Way* will give you practical ideas and insights on servant leadership and will fill your heart—and *that* is where the servant leadership Jesus taught always begins!"

—Todd Gongwer
Author, Lead For God's Sake

"There are thousands of books about leadership but this is the one you need to read! Embracing Mark's Model of Servant Leadership outlined in *Leading Jesus' Way* will transform your life. You can be an effective leader and care about the people you lead by learning how to serve them first."

—Lynette Kluver
V.P. Organization Development, Alexandria Industries

"Mark's ability to teach and draw upon servant leadership as modeled by Jesus Christ is outstanding. The principles he shares in *Leading Jesus' Way* have significantly impacted all aspects of my life and leadership…at home, in business and within my community. I'm confident it will have the same impact on you!"

—Jeremy Duininck
Vice President, Prinsco

"Reading *Leading Jesus' Way* will move your focus from success to significance. It has taught me how my role as an executive leader can have a life changing positive impact on those around me. By following the servant leadership principles outlined in *Leading Jesus' Way*, you will become a more effective leader as well as gain personal fulfillment in your life and career."

—Michael Murphy
Chief Performance Officer, Trend Offset Printing Services, Inc.

"The principles in *Leading Jesus' Way* have been the foundation for the transition of our family business from one generation to the next. The biblical principles shared in such practical, user-friendly teachings are so welcoming to all. Your only regret in embracing servant leadership in your personal and professional life will be that you didn`t have it earlier in your journey."

—Tim Cullen
President, Cullen's Home Center

"The servant leadership principles in *Leading Jesus' Way* are life changing. Gaining God's perspective for the purpose of my life as a servant leader has provided the prospective, energy and focus to make a true difference in my personal and professional life. You will be blessed by leading Jesus' way!"

—Peter Nelson
President, Glenwood State Bank

"Mark outlines a compelling model of servant leadership based on scripture, thoughtful insight and years of proven servant leadership. *Leading Jesus' Way* will challenge you to understand and embrace the servant leadership Jesus modeled. Get the book! You will be inspired and energized to invest in your character, talent and faith to improve your performance, grow your relationships and transform your leadership."

—Mike Henry Sr.
Chief Instigator, Lead Change Group

"I've worked closely with Mark over the last several years. The servant leadership principles that he so clearly outlines in *Leading Jesus' Way* have helped me understand my personal life purpose, and how we drive a culture of servant leadership at Knute Nelson. By leading Jesus' way our leaders have strengthened our culture beyond measure to grow our capacities to serve and live out our mission."

—Mark Anderson
President & CEO, Knute Nelson

"The exposure to the servant leadership principles in *Leading Jesus' Way* has been a life changing experience for me. After 30 plus years in my career I think I am starting to "get it." Focusing on serving people as a leader will make an amazing impact on your life."

—Al Sholts
Chief Operating Officer, Alexandria Industries

"Following the game plan outlined in *Leading Jesus' Way* has provided just the right boost for my personal life, and has transformed our organization. You will find working through this book as a team will lead to eye-opening truths of what it means to be a servant leader and will build accountability to becoming the servant leader that God created you to be."

—Stuart Giere
Engineering Manager, Nova-Tech Engineering

"Mark's model of servant leadership outlined in *Leading Jesus' Way* has had a tremendous impact on my life, as well as on Douglas Machine. Our leaders have experienced a transformation into leading with a servant's heart and leading from the bottom up instead of directing. This way of leadership, which comes out of caring for people, is absolutely amazing and will have a positive impact for years to come."

—Vern Anderson
Chairman, Douglas Machine Inc.
Unity Foundation, Alexandria, MN

"I have had the privilege of attending Mark's teachings on Servant leadership in community settings, businesses, church oversight teams, a family portrait weekend, and as a personal coach. My wife continues to testify that our weekend with Mark, establishing our Family Portrait, is still the most important weekend of our many years of marriage. *Leading Jesus' Way* will empower you to have a greater understanding of the influence servant leadership can have on your life."

—Doug Wing
Senior Pastor, Grace Life Church, Marshall, MN

"Leading Jesus' Way: Become the Leader God Created You to Be is titled appropriately. This is one of the best primers on servant leadership I have read. Mark Deterding invites his readers into the experience of learning what it means to be an authentic leader who models the life and leadership style of Jesus Christ.

Functioning as a playbook for servant leadership, it lays out a tactical plan for building your organization, team, or family on a foundation of moral integrity, solid character, and strong faith. As a coach would lead a team, Mark walks readers through chapters that are building blocks of each other, stopping along the way for review and practical exercises.

Mark draws upon his extensive background as a corporate leader, entrepreneur, and leadership coach to help you understand the unique role of servant leadership and be able to put into practice the disciplines integrated into a servant leadership culture."

—Jane Anderson,
Social Media Strategist
Insite Skill Inc.

LEADING
JESUS'
WAY

Become The
Servant Leader
God Created
You To Be

Mark Deterding

Copyright © 2016 by Mark Deterding.

All rights reserved. No part of this publication may be reproduced, distributed or transmitted in any form or by any means, without prior written permission.

Weaving Influence, Inc.
6530 Secor Road, Suite 7
Lambertville, MI 48144

weavinginfluence.com

Leading Jesus' Way: Become the Servant Leader God Created You to Be by Mark Deterding. — 1st ed.

Print Edition ISBN 978-0692755532

DEDICATION

To my Lord and Savior Jesus Christ who modeled servant leadership so effectively, all the way to providing the ultimate sacrifice for me.

To my wife, Kim, for her never-ending support and encouragement in my endeavors to spread the word on servant leadership to positively impact the world. She is a daily model of servant leadership for me.

To my children, David and Dan, and their families who are just as passionate about servant leadership as I am, and inspire me through their never-ending love.

To my parents who were my life-long role models of servant leadership, even though they never used the term "servant leadership".

To my coaching clients who inspire me daily with their heart and passion for servant leadership and their desire to positively change the world.

To all those who read *Leading Jesus' Way* for their desire to look to the ultimate role model of servant leadership to help them become the leader that God created them to be.

CONTENTS

FOREWORD

WARNING! *Leading Jesus' Way: Become the Servant Leader God Created You to Be* is a most dangerous book! If you read this book, be ready to radically change your life and your approach to leadership. I know this because I know Mark and I've experienced what can happen when you put his servant leadership model to work.

I got to know Mark when he joined the board at the Unity Foundation, a Christian organization in Alexandria, MN that is focused on letting God out of the box in the workplace.

Mark had a very successful career in the printing industry, starting on the shop floor and working his way up to the top. All the principles in this book are things he learned on the shop floor, in the office, in his plants around the country, as well as through his study of God's Word. He showed the people who worked for him a way to lead that not only would positively impact the company but also positively impact their lives.

That's the proof in the pudding for me. I want to hear from a guy that actually sat in the leader's chair and built high performing teams and organizations in the most challenging times. He truly illustrated that servant leadership works!

Even though he was successful, Mark left the company he was with for 20+ years for a reason I truly respect. Ownership changed and Mark didn't feel that their values and his were in alignment any longer. That doesn't happen often and it impressed me. But I was soon even more impressed with his deep knowledge of servant leadership.

As we worked together on the Unity board, Mark was constantly sharing what he'd learned about servant leadership. He wasn't talking theory, he shared what he'd done and how it worked and he had a gift for helping you understand how to use it. Several of us encouraged Mark to make sharing his concepts of faith-based servant leadership the next phase of his career.

I'm the CEO of Alexandria Industries. We're a privately held company with about 650 employees and plants in three states. When Mark was starting his firm, we were about two to three years into a strategic planning process. We had read about servant leadership and it resonated with our values, but it was very abstract and we couldn't see how to institutionalize it at our company.

I thought that Mark could help us, so I brought him in and, boy, was that a great decision. He helped us clarify our purpose and values, and then helped us understand how servant leadership was the best way to live them. Mark took servant leadership from an abstract concept to a practical business tool.

Mark has trained people in all our plants. We've incorporated servant leadership into the programs in our Leadership Academy. It hasn't only changed how we do business, it's changed our lives.

I know it's changed my life, and I'm sure I could go around the senior leadership table and every one of the people would say the same thing. It's changed how we act with our families as well as how we act with people at work. The results have been extraordinary. Let me share three examples.

There's an engineer who's been with us for more than thirty years. He went through Leadership Roundtable, which is the program this book is based on. I remember standing with him in the parking lot, while he shared how excited he was about what he had learned. He told me, "It's changed my life, changed my marriage, changed how I react to my grown children, changed my work."

Here's another one. I was walking around the plant when one of our third shift supervisors stopped me. He had been through the servant leadership training and changed the way he did his job. That man showed me a letter from one of the people who work for him. Here's part of it: "Steve,

I love working for you. I've never had a boss that cares so much about me and is willing to do what you've done for me." I tell you, I had tears running down my face that day.

I've also observed senior executives, people who've been top performers for decades, start to take more of an interest in developing their people because of the training and Mark's coaching. That means we're doing a better job of retaining and developing people who will be running this company long after I'm gone.

Thank God that this is a way that we can help our people, but thank God it's also a way where we can be the most successful company that there ever can be. We don't have to give up our performance from a metrics standpoint because we're using servant leadership. The absolute opposite is true.

I've probably gone on too long, so here's the bottom line. This is a solid, practical book about how you can lead more effectively and make a positive difference in people's lives. It's also based on the scriptures and Jesus' example. It will truly help you lead Jesus' way.

Tom Schabel
CEO, Alexandria Industries
Alexandria MN
June 10, 2016

PREFACE

Looking back, it seems like everything in my life prepared me to write this book.

I became really interested in the Bible when I was a junior in high school. I was fascinated with the gospels and the way Jesus lived. That's also when prayer became a big part of my life.

When I was playing baseball, for example, I prayed before every time I stepped up to bat. I developed the habit of leaning on Jesus and I experienced the great things that can happen when you do.

My Mom and Dad were great role models. They served their children and everyone around them, too. They set the standard for what I wanted to become.

I had the opportunity to work at the same printing company as my dad and I noticed how he led by serving others. I've spent my whole career working to live up to his standard. He respected everyone and constantly made comments that would build people up, but he always made sure that the work was done right. I think that's where I got my passion for building high performing teams.

Through thirty-five years of leading thousands of people in the printing business, I had the opportunity to learn what works and what doesn't work from a leadership standpoint. I learned a lot from many great role models. You'll read more about them in the book.

I learned a lot, but I never connected it to my Bible study until the early 2000s. I've got all kinds of notes in my Bible about the leadership behaviors that Jesus demonstrates. I started to realize that Jesus was the best leadership role model.

2005 was an important growth year for me. I was working with my culture coach, Chris Edmonds, and learning how to create a purpose-driven, values-based culture. I was also connecting what I learned with my growing understanding of how to live out my faith at work.

I think that's when I started using the term "servant leadership" to describe what I was doing and the kind of culture I wanted to create. Around this time, I read books on servant leadership such as Ken Blanchard's Lead Like Jesus and Leadership by the Book.

I built a model that resonated with my experience and study. I knew that Jesus was the perfect role model for a way of leading that got great results and changed people's lives. My father demonstrated those principles in his life. And I'd used them in my own career, from the shop floor all the way to the job where I was responsible for a billion-dollar business, with ten business unit presidents as my direct reports.

I knew that servant leadership wasn't a set of "soft" practices. I learned that it requires serious discipline and commitment. And it's not just about making people feel good. Servant leadership certainly boosted the bottom line for the businesses I led. You'll read about the details in the book. Even so, I went looking for research to see if my experience was typical.

I found research by Dr. James Sipe who's now a Managing Principal with Korn Ferry International. Dr. Sipe compared the before-tax profits of "servant-led" companies with all the companies on the S & P 500 for the ten years from 1994 – 2004. The S&P companies generated 10.2 percent pre-tax profit. Servant-led companies more than doubled that with pre-tax profits of 24.2 percent.

I was excited about what I'd learned about servant leadership. I looked forward to using what I'd learned for the rest of my career. But God had other plans.

The company where I worked for years changed hands. The new owners had different priorities and values than I did. I realized that the servant leadership skills I'd developed over decades and that were now part of the way I lived out my Christian faith were not aligned with the way the new owners wanted things done. I left the company, without a clear idea of what I was going to do next.

I prayed for guidance. But I was pretty sure God wanted me to do more than pray, so I worked with some local organizations while I got my feet on the ground and figured out what was next.

I serve on the board of the Unity Foundation where our purpose is "to encourage sharing the Christian faith in the workplace." Three people in particular from that board, Vern Anderson, Tim Cullen, and Tom Schabel pushed me to make spreading the word about servant leadership the focus of the next phase of my life. They helped me make Triune Leadership a successful undertaking.

We did our first Leadership Roundtable program in 2010. I knew that servant leadership got results and changed people's lives. What I wanted to create with the Roundtables was a model for how to step into servant leadership, real practical advice that any leader can use to make servant leadership work.

Leadership Roundtables consist of one three-hour session a month for seven months. They're designed to help participants understand and use the principles of servant leadership. The Roundtables gave me real-world experience in making the principles usable and lots of great feedback about how to do it better.

Now I had a whole package. I had the lessons I personally learned using faith-based servant leadership to get results in the companies where I worked. I had learned from other writers about servant leadership. I had unearthed solid research supporting the potential of servant leadership in a business. And I had a field-tested way to help other people put what I had learned to work. There was still one more challenge.

I want to expand the message beyond my physical ability to be in front of people, so I wrote *Leading Jesus' Way*. It has taken me more than two years to get it right.

It is my heart that when you read this book you will gain the courage and tools to live out your faith at work and become a more effective and impactful leader. I hope that you share what you have learned. That's how we can make a difference today and leave the world a better place for future generations. I'm inspired by this passage from Paul's letter to the Romans.

"For everything that was written in the past was written to teach us, so that through the endurance taught in the Scriptures and the encouragement they provide we might have hope."

Enjoy your journey!

Mark Deterding
Alexandria, MN
June 2016

INTRODUCTION

What kind of leader did God create me to be?

Every day Ron goes to work and asks himself that question. Ron is the owner of a successful business. Dozens of people work for him, and he wants to do the right thing for them, for the business, and for his customers. So he wonders: "What does it mean to be a Christian if you're the CEO?" Consuelo asks similar questions.

Consuelo is an engineer who works in the company where Ron is the CEO. She doesn't have a leadership position, but she's a team member on a lot of projects. Sometimes she's the project team leader. She's not sure how to act when she has an idea she thinks is important. She wants to be the humble person she thinks God wants her to be, but she also wants to speak up about ideas she thinks will help the team perform better.

Most of us spend more than half our waking hours at work. And most of us want to live out our faith at work. That's what this book is about.

Leading Jesus' Way is a manual for bringing your Christian faith to work. In the pages that follow, you'll find practical concepts and tools to help you be the leader who makes a difference for others, whatever position you hold.

A 16th Century poem by St. Teresa of Avila includes the following words: "Yours are the hands, yours are the feet, yours are the eyes, you are his body, Christ has no body now but yours." This tells me that if God's work is going to be done on Earth, it is up to me.

So what does God want from me? He wants me to use the gifts He has given me to the fullest. That's the message of Romans 12:6–8. Here it is in the NIV translation.

> We have different gifts, according to the grace given to each of us. If your gift is prophesying, then prophesy in accordance with your faith; if it is serving, then serve; if it is teaching, then teach; if it is to encourage, then give encouragement; if it is giving, then give generously; if it is to lead, do it diligently; if it is to show mercy, do it cheerfully.

Obviously, some people have the gifts to be preachers and teachers and missionaries. Some have the gifts to be doctors and nurses, healers and caregivers. Most of us have other gifts. My gifts are in business.

I started my first business when I was in the fourth grade. At the time jumbo eggs weren't available in most stores. I hooked up with a farmer to sell jumbo eggs to families in town, delivered fresh to their door.

Throughout my high school and college years I worked at a printing plant, and my first job out of college was at a nationally renowned web offset magazine and catalog printing company. For over thirty years I advanced in the companies I worked for until I was responsible for thousands of people and over a billion dollars in annual revenue. I learned how to do business well, and I also learned how to put my faith to work.

I was blessed to have opportunities and many wise people who helped me. I made a lot of mistakes and I tried to learn from them. Many people told me that if you wanted to be successful in business, you had to compromise your principles and your Christian faith.

I discovered that wasn't true at all. I learned that I was a better leader and a better business person when I used the scriptures to guide me. I learned that I was a better leader when I followed the principles described by Ezekiel in 571 BC.

He described the difference between bad shepherds and good shepherds. They are the same as the differences between a self-serving leader and a servant leader.

Bad shepherds:

» Take care of themselves
» Worry about their own health and safety
» Rule harshly and brutally
» Abandon the sheep
» Keep the best for themselves

Good shepherds:

» Take care of their flock
» Strengthen the weak and sick, and search for the lost
» Rule lovingly and gently
» Gather and protect the sheep
» Give their best to their sheep

Ezekiel was writing about the leaders of Israel in his day. He was also describing the best model for servant leadership, the Lord Jesus Christ.

The good shepherds that Ezekiel described were more effective shepherds. They lost fewer sheep to predators and accidents and disease. The sheep they took to market were fatter and healthier and fetched a better price. Good shepherd leaders do better today, too.

Right now you may be thinking, "That's fine if you're the CEO or if you own the company. What about the rest of us? We don't have an important position like that. We're just ordinary people." The fact is, we're all ordinary people. And another fact is, you can be a leader no matter what job you have.

There are dozens, maybe even hundreds, of definitions of what makes a leader. There's only one thing they all agree on. *Leaders have followers.* Leaders have other people who pay attention to what they say and do so they can be better themselves.

True, some leaders are like Ron. Their position makes them responsible for results for a few or for thousands of people. But Consuelo can be a leader, too.

She doesn't need to be the leader. She doesn't have to lead all the time. But there are times when she needs to step up and speak up, to help her team perform better.

Leading is nothing more complicated than consciously influencing the behavior of others. No matter what position you have in your company or in life, you have opportunities to lead. I wrote this book to help you make the best of those opportunities. It's about faith-based servant leadership.

Faith-based servant leadership is rooted in the Christian faith and based on scriptural principles. It's based on Jesus' words to the disciples in Mark, "Anyone who wants to be first must be the very last, and the servant of all."

The good news is that there's a proven way to make the journey from where you are now to effective, faith-based servant leadership.

After I left my last executive position, I founded Triune Leadership Services *to awaken the servant hearts within leaders and equip them to make a significant positive impact on the world.* We do this in a number of ways.

I work with executive teams as a Certified Leadership Development consultant to equip them with the principles and tools of servant leaders and provide a process to help them institutionalize a servant-leadership culture. I conduct Servant Leadership Roundtables to provide those same benefits to anyone who wants to become a more effective, faith-based servant leader. I am also an Executive Coach for leaders who want to accelerate their progress in areas they want to improve.

This isn't magic; it takes effort and commitment and time. Sometimes it's difficult. But we know it works because, since 2011, hundreds of people have participated in our Servant Leadership Roundtables and learned how to become leaders who make a difference.

They learned how to bring their faith to work. They learned how to use scriptural principles to do a better job of what they do. They learned how to use the example of Jesus Christ to become effective, faith-based servant leaders. You can learn those things, too. Following is an overview of the model.

THE TRIUNE LEADERSHIP MODEL OF SERVANT LEADERSHIP

Recently, my wife and I took an amazing cruise to Alaska. Before we even decided to go, we reviewed travel brochures and websites to get an idea of what the trip would be like. This chapter is like a travel brochure that will give you a brief overview of what your journey to faith-based servant leadership will be like.

You're going to learn a model that has worked for me while leading organizations. It has worked for my coaching and leadership development clients. And it has worked for the hundreds of people who have participated in Servant Leadership Roundtables.

Our experience tells us that this model works. When you have worked your way through it, you will be able to do a better job of consciously influencing the behavior of others. Many leadership programs can make that claim. But this model is also faith-based.

The model is faith-based because it uses biblical principles to guide your leadership. Our work is empowered by the Holy Spirit, and we use Jesus Christ as the model of a perfect leader.

If you're like many people I speak with, you may not ever have thought of Jesus Christ as a leadership role model. Frankly, I think that's because most of the people speaking and writing about Jesus are pastors and teachers. It's only natural that they see the Lord through the lens of their own work. But I'm a businessperson, and I look at the Lord through a leadership lens.

When I do that, I see that Jesus was the perfect leadership model. In just three years' time, He put together a team of men who would carry His message to the world and change it. They didn't just "buy in"; they were willing to die for their faith. Tradition tells us that only one of the disciples died of natural causes. The rest were martyred.

That's powerful leadership. And when we study what Jesus did as a leader, we learn lessons that help us do better. I've learned those lessons from studying scripture, and I've learned them from the wisdom that other believers have shared with me. Most importantly, I learned from trying to put the lessons to work.

I've attended a lot of leadership training in my life, and I've read a lot of leadership books. Far too often, I discovered I hadn't learned enough to use the lessons when I was "in the chair." As far as possible, I want to give you tools you can use so you can be the leader the Lord wants you to be.

Leadership is a doing discipline. It's not like studying history, it's like learning to swim or ride a bike. You have to do it to learn it. That means you'll get some of it wrong, but that's okay, if you learn from it.

Some of what you will learn won't make sense when you read it. It may contradict things you've learned about leadership before. That's normal. It happens for everyone. That's when I hope you'll act like the publican in Mark 2:14. Here's the verse.

> As he walked along, he saw Levi son of Alphaeus sitting at the
> tax collector's booth. "Follow me," Jesus told him, and Levi got
> up and followed him.

Levi didn't ask for an explanation. He got up, left all his belongings behind and followed Jesus. You won't have to do anything so drastic, but you will probably leave some of your old beliefs and practices behind.

There's one more thing you should know about our model of faith-based servant leadership. It's a system.

The Merriam-Webster Dictionary defines a system as "a regularly interacting or interdependent group of items forming a unified whole." Your car's air conditioner is a system.

There are many different parts to the system. There are controls and hoses and a compressor and a fan and more. When all the parts are working together, the air conditioning system works. But if you remove one of the parts, you don't get less air conditioning. You get no air conditioning. For a system to work, all the parts must be working and they must be working together.

Our model of faith-based servant leadership is a system with five parts. Here's a quick description of each one in the order you will experience them.

BUILD THE FOUNDATION

Remember the wise and foolish builders from Matthew chapter 7? You will build a strong foundation to support everything else. The foundation for faith-based servant leadership is your purpose, vision, and values.

BUILD ENERGY

You want to lead with energy and help others engage energetically in achieving the purpose and vision. You will learn five key elements of building energy.

BUILD PERFORMANCE

Knowing your purpose, vision, and values is essential. Acting with energy is great. But unless you produce results, it's all a mental exercise. Performance matters.

BUILD RELATIONSHIPS

There isn't much more important in a faith-based servant leader's life than relationships. Building relationships is often the difference between a good leader and a great one. The quality of the relationships is what separates other leaders from servant leaders. In this section, you'll review six powerful ways to build relationships.

BUILD YOUR PERSONAL CHARACTER

You are never done working to become a better faith-based servant leader. You will develop your skills, but the most important work you do will be on your character. You will never finish developing your skills and deepening your faith and understanding. This section will give you some ways to continue developing your character.

That's just an overview. Your journey starts in the next chapter.

GETTING THE MOST FROM THIS BOOK

Before you turn the page, you may want to download the "Learning Materials" specifically crafted to help you get the most out of reading and applying, *Leading Jesus' Way.*

Simply visit www.leadingjesusway.com to access your free materials and enter pass-code: servantleadership (case sensitive).

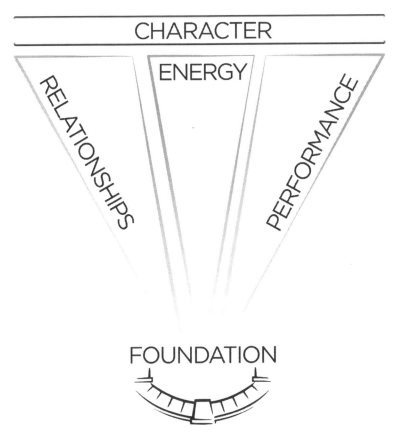

© Triune Leadership Services, LLC Please Do Not Duplicate.

BUILD THE FOUNDATION

INTRODUCTION

My wife Kim and I love the outdoors. We love to hike, and when we go on vacation we seek out destinations with good hiking. One of our favorites is Sedona, Arizona.

Sedona is in the high desert. There are magnificent sandstone formations and some of the most spectacular thunderstorms you could ever want to see. The lightning can be dangerous, but the thunderstorms bring another danger, too. Those big storms can generate flash floods that make me think of the famous verses from Matthew 7:24–27 (NIV).

Therefore everyone who hears these words of mine and puts them into practice is like a wise man who built his house on the rock. The rain came down, the streams rose, and the winds blew and beat against that house; yet it did not fall, because it had its foundation on the rock. But everyone who hears these words of mine and does not put them into practice is like a foolish man who built his house on sand. The rain came down, the streams rose, and the winds blew and beat against that house, and it fell with a great crash.

When I read that passage, I think Matthew is describing flash floods in the desert. They hit with a power that can destroy anything that isn't built with the very strongest foundation. This section is about building a strong foundation for your leadership, one that can withstand the powerful forces that the world will hurl against you.

The three components of your foundation will be your *purpose*, your *values*, and your *vision*. They are the building blocks for a foundation that will help you create a structure of faith-based servant leadership.

In the next chapter you'll do the work to discover your purpose. Your purpose is *why* you put your feet on the floor in the morning.

Following that you'll work through how your values impact your daily life. Your values define *how* you should behave to remain true to your purpose.

The final chapter in this section is where you'll craft your vision. Your vision will define *what* you want to accomplish.

There are some things you should understand as you work through these chapters. The first is that it starts with you.

I believe that personal mastery leads to professional mastery. You need to understand your own personal purpose, values, and vision before you attempt to influence the world around you. Your personal purpose, values, and vision provide a base on which to build the foundation for any subsequent group you are leading.

Other examples where a foundation would be appropriate might be:

» Your family
» A team you are leading or coaching
» A department you are responsible for
» Your company
» Areas of your church that you are leading

If you're the designated leader of a group, you have a special challenge. Whether you're a CEO like Ron, a temporary project leader like Consuelo, or even a Sunday School teacher, you have a special kind of influence. I learned about it very early in my career.

I noticed that if I made a casual suggestion while walking around the plant, people acted on it. Just about everyone I've ever talked to who's had positional authority has noticed this phenomenon. Sometimes it's amusing to watch.

One young friend was so anxious to get to work on the first day of his new management job that he forgot to make his habitual stop for a morning cup of coffee. When someone on his new team asked him how his day was going, he mentioned forgetting his coffee. Within a couple of minutes a team member brought him the cup of coffee he hadn't really asked for.

God seems to have wired us to defer to authority. Watch how people choose seats the next time you go to a meeting. I bet that no one except the nominal leader will take the seat at the head of the table.

That kind of power can be seductive. As faith-based servant leaders, we have to struggle against the temptation to take charge and to act like we're important. We have to be *servant* leaders.

But there is at least one case when it's your job to use that power humbly. If you are senior leadership, it's part of your job to help establish the Foundation for the group.

Building the foundation is hard work. Building your personal foundation requires time, reflection, prayer, and a lot of hard thinking. Developing an organization or team foundation also takes time, discussion with your leadership team, and real understanding of your organization and environment.

I know you want to get started right away, but I hope you'll do two things first:

» Take a moment to write down all the areas of your life in which you are a leader. Doing that now will help you be more effective as you work through the following chapters.
» Pray for God's guidance as you develop your foundations.

DETERMINING YOUR PURPOSE

For even the Son of Man did not come to be served,
but to serve, and to give his life as a ransom for many.
Mark 10:45 (NIV)

This passage is all you need to understand about Jesus' actions through His entire time on Earth. Imagine that you were there, in Galilee, where Jesus' ministry on Earth played out. You would have seen a powerful teacher and leader.

Jesus taught "as one with authority." His preaching drew crowds so big, He had to get into a boat and go out on the water to be able to teach them. He could have hobnobbed with the rich and the powerful, but He chose to set an example of serving. Jesus chose to do things that were part of His purpose and avoid things that were not.

He could have led the rebellion so many of His followers wanted. He did not. That was not His purpose. He could have assumed the trappings and rewards of power. He did not. That was not His purpose either. When the time came to go up to Jerusalem and submit to His fate at the hands of the powerful, He could have turned away. He did not.

Giving His life "as a ransom for many," including you and me, was a part of His purpose. This chapter is about discerning *your* purpose so you can use it to guide your life and your leadership.

THE ANSWER TO THE BIG QUESTION

"Why do *I* exist?" That's the big question we all need to answer. I'm not talking about a formal, detailed, philosophical answer. Your purpose is something simpler and more basic.

When you think about your personal purpose, answer the question, "Why do I get out of bed in the morning?" When you know your personal purpose, you will move though your day with energy and focus. When you know your purpose, you will discover that many of life's decisions are easier to make. Let me share an example you've probably heard of.

WHY DETERMINING YOUR PURPOSE IS IMPORTANT

One reason purpose is important is that, when you know your purpose, it makes decisions easier. Let's consider the case of Southwest Airlines.

Southwest Airlines is an airline phenomenon. They started in 1971. Their first profitable year was 1973. In an industry where bankruptcies and unprofitable years are the norm, Southwest Airlines has been profitable every year since 1973. Knowing their purpose is part of the reason.

When Southwest Airlines began operating about 40 years ago, they determined that their purpose was *to open up the airways to everybody, not just the wealthy.* Knowing their purpose helped them make all kinds of decisions.

If you want to make air travel something almost anyone can do, it makes sense to have low fares. To be able to offer low fares and still be profitable, Southwest had to find ways to operate more efficiently than other airlines.

They decided to fly only one kind of plane. That made almost all their operations more efficient. It reduced the need for several maintenance hubs. It cut out crew scheduling hassles, because every crew member is qualified on every airplane Southwest flies.

When they started the business, about 18 percent of the American public had flown on a commercial airline. Today it's over 90 percent. Southwest Airlines is a big part of the reasons why. But here's what's important for our purposes.

Southwest Airlines could make all kinds of strategic and operational decisions easily because they knew their purpose. When you get locked down on your purpose, it will help you in every decision that you've got to make in your life, personally, professionally and with any organization.

You ask one simple question: "Is this decision going to help advance my purpose or not?" I've answered this question both ways in my own life.

I left a major job because we had had a change in ownership and the new owners had a purpose that made it impossible for me to stay and still live out my purpose. Knowing my purpose made it clear to me that I could not stay at that company.

Knowing your purpose gives you another benefit besides easier decision making. *Knowing your purpose leads to working with passion.* That's the situation I'm in now.

My personal purpose is *to glorify God by helping leaders to lead at a higher level and enable them to achieve their God-given potential.* That purpose is the passion that drives me through my days. I was fortunate to be able to start my company, Triune Leadership Services, and define the purpose of the organization around my personal purpose. Most people aren't in that situation.

Consider Stephen Lynch from New Zealand. At one point in his life, he was the top salesperson and then the top sales manager for a pharmaceutical company. He enjoyed the work and the people he worked with, but something was missing for him.

He had defined his purpose when he was working toward the Mr. New Zealand bodybuilding title. He discerned that his purpose was *to help people set goals and achieve them.* The pharmaceutical jobs were good ones, but they didn't help him live his purpose. The pharmaceutical had a noble purpose, but it wasn't the same as Stephen's.

So he left the pharmaceutical company. Now he's with a consulting firm whose purpose is to help small to midsized businesses to be successful. Stephen's personal purpose fits with the firm's purpose. Being able to live out his purpose every day gives him energy and focus.

If you're the leader of a company or a team, you want people like that. Successful organizations have people who can't wait to get in to work. That's because they are going after a purpose that is very important and that is above and beyond their paycheck, and they can't wait to get after it.

When you have an organization with a really compelling purpose, that's exactly what will happen. People will be racing to work because they know they will be able to give their full energy and attention to something that fulfills their purpose.

The first thing you need to do is discern your personal purpose. I believe that personal mastery leads to professional mastery. When you understand your own purpose, you can see how you fit with your family or the place where you work.

THE THREE COMPONENTS OF PURPOSE

When you have your personal purpose framed up, you will live your life with energy and focus. Your purpose will have three components: *what you do, for whom you do it, and why.* Those three core elements are what will make up your purpose, whether it's your personal purpose, your professional purpose, your family purpose, or your organization's purpose. Here's how it looks in my purpose: *Glorify God, as I help people to perform and lead at a higher level, and enable them to achieve their God-given potential.*

HOW TO DISCERN YOUR PURPOSE

After spending several years helping people with this, I believe that you don't create your own purpose. You discern your purpose. In the religious world you might say that it's figuring out your "Calling from God." Let me put it in more earthly terms. You've been gifted with skills and talents; there are things you are passionate about and that you think are important. When you analyze how those things work in your life, you're on your way to discerning your purpose.

I have found the following steps to be effective when discerning your personal purpose:

1. Pray for God's guidance on the process, trusting that He will provide clarity on His mission for you while on earth.
2. Document your personal strengths, skills, and talents that God has gifted you with.
3. Document those things that you value highly and/or hold sacred.
4. Prioritize these two lists and then determine what you are *most* passionate about.
5. Document what you want to be remembered for (your legacy).
6. Considering these reflections, put together a *purpose statement* that illustrates who you are, what you value, what you are going to provide, and for what reason this will be done.

That's an overview. Here are those same steps, with a little more detail.

This Foundation Section takes a lot of work. You may find it helpful to download the Forms Packet from the web site.

Pray for God's guidance on the process, trusting that He will provide clarity on His mission for you while on earth. Prayer is the way we connect our lives to God's will. We believe that when we ask He will answer and when we seek He will help us find our way. That is why we pray for guidance when discerning our purpose.

Warning: You will be tempted to see this process as several discrete steps that you do one after the other. The process works best if you go back and forth and over and over the next three steps.

Suggestion: Make some notes about each one and then go about your daily routine. Keep some index cards or a notebook or a digital voice recorder handy to capture any ideas you get about your strengths or what's important. Add those insights to your notes.

If you spend a few days doing this, you'll gain more insight into yourself and your strengths and the things you think are important.

Document your personal strengths, skills, and talents that God has gifted you with. You can do several things to help identify your strengths. Write down the things people tell you you're good at. Write down things you do easily and well, but other people seem to find more difficult. Ask your friends what they think are your strengths. One way to do that is to email several of them and ask them to tell you about a time when they think you were at your best.

Be sure to take time for prayerful reflection. Ask yourself what tasks you "get lost in," where time seems to fly by. What tasks give you energy?

Document those things that you value highly and/or hold sacred. What's most important to you? Take a look at how you spend your money. Review your calendar. How do you spend your time? Try completing the following sentence:

It's a good day when …

Prioritize these two lists and then determine what, between the two lists, you are most passionate about. There are no rules about how to do this, so choose any method that works for you. When you're done, you're almost there, but there's a little more work to do.

Document what you want to be remembered for (your legacy). Think about what you would like people to say about you at your memorial service. What kinds of stories do you want your friends and loved ones to tell about you?

Considering these reflections, put together a purpose statement that illustrates who you are, what you value, what you are going to provide, and for what reason this will be done. I've already shared my purpose statement with you. Here are some other people's purpose statements that I like a lot.

To be a student and teacher of simple truths.
—Ken Blanchard

To serve as a leader, live a balanced life, and apply ethical principles to make a significant difference.
—Denise Morrison, CEO, Campbell Soup

Lift people up, make Jesus smile.
—Brent Smith, CEO, Aagard Group

Your purpose will not necessarily be directly tied to your profession or job. Look at those statements you just read. Your purpose will be applicable to all aspects of your life and can be carried out every day, wherever you happen to be.

Your purpose is important, but simply knowing your purpose is not enough. To live the life God wants you to live, you need to think about how to act so your actions and your purpose are aligned. Your values define how you should act so you remain true to your purpose.

DEFINING AND LIVING YOUR VALUES

I have set you an example that you should do as I have done for you. Very truly I tell you, no servant is greater than his master, nor is a messenger greater than the one who sent him. Now that you know these things, you will be blessed if you do them.
~ John 13:15–17 (NIV)

You may be puzzling over why I chose that Bible verse for a chapter on values. You may believe that values are mental things, things that live inside us. That's true. In fact, it's the dictionary definition of *values*, like this from *dictionary.com:*

> a person's principles or standards of behavior; one's judgment of what is important in life.

Those judgments are important but they're only the start, because the things we really value are the things we act out. In his book, *The One That Got Away,* Howell Raines writes about legendary Alabama football coach Paul "Bear" Bryant. I love what he said: "Coach Bryant had an idea about how a man should act, and if you watched him you could figure it out."

How we act is important. How we spend our time and our money tells the world what we really think is important. So does the way we treat others. You've probably heard the song, "They Will Know We Are Christians by Our Love." That's what values are all about: what we think is important and how we act based on that.

WHAT QUESTION YOUR VALUES ANSWER

Your personal values answer the question, "How should I behave?" Your organizational values answer the question, "How should we behave?" We'll tackle personal values first.

Values are your enduring beliefs that you seek to attain. At a personal level we use the term *values*. When we talk about the same thing in organizations we usually use the term *culture*.

Another way to think of values is that your values are what you want to be known for. When people think of you, what do you want them to say? How do you want them to describe you?

You may want people to think of you as a good parent. That's a value. Perhaps you want people to say that they can trust you or that you're a Christian or you're a loyal friend. Those are values, too. Knowing what you value is important, but it isn't enough.

WHY JUST KNOWING YOUR VALUES IS NOT ENOUGH

When we evaluate other people, we don't evaluate them on the values that are inside their head. We don't have any way of knowing what those values are. So we look at their behavior: what they say and what they do. Of those two kinds of behavior, we pay the most attention to what another person does and whether what they say and what they do are in alignment.

Other people evaluate you the same way. They can't see inside your head and know what your values are. So they'll listen to what you say and watch what you do, and they will pay the most attention to what you do.

We've all known people who said they were Christians but didn't act like it. They could recite Bible verses for any situation. They talked a good game, but the talk and the walk didn't match up.

If you want to live a life based on your values, you have to determine what values matter the most to you. Then you have to define the behaviors that are consistent with those values. That way, other people will be able to tell what really matters to you. Knowing how to act will also help you remain aware of how you *should* act. Here's an example.

I have a personal value that I call "Well-Being of Body, Mind, and Spirit." Part of that is being healthy. I know that if I want to be healthy, I have to do certain things every day to stay healthy. A few years ago I added back exercises to my list.

It happened after I found myself lying flat on the floor, unable to get up. Physicians and therapists helped me fix the issue, but they also wanted me to stay healthy, so they gave me a set of back exercises. I do them every morning, religiously.

Doing morning back exercises is a behavior that supports my "Well-Being of Body, Mind, and Spirit" value. Because I've defined it, I can tell every day if I'm doing the things I need to do to support that value.

When you know your values and define them behaviorally, you will live them. Other people will see what you do and know what's important for you. And evaluating your own behavior can be a daily test of whether you are doing things that support your values.

HOW TO DEFINE YOUR KEY VALUES

You can define your key values with the three-step process we use at our Leadership Roundtables:

1. Choose a few words that describe a key value for you.
2. Define the value in a sentence or two.
3. Describe the behaviors that support the value.

To help you with this, we've included a Forms Packet on our website. The forms are in PDF format so you can download them and print them easily.

Choose a Few Words That Describe a Key Value for You

The first step is to come up with a word or two. Here's a list of possibilities that we use in our Leadership Roundtables. They're also on the Personal Values Worksheet in the Forms Packet.

Value Words

Ambition	Competency	Individuality	Integrity
Service	Responsibility	Accuracy	Respect
Dedication	Excellence	Trust	Diversity
Improvement	Enjoyment / Fun	Loyalty	Credibility
Honesty	Innovativeness	Teamwork	Accountability
Quality	Efficiency	Dignity	Stewardship
Collaboration	Empathy	Courage	Wisdom
Independence	Security	Challenge	Influence
Learning	Compassion	Friendliness	Generosity
Discipline	Persistency	Optimism	Flexibility
Health	Peace	Patience	Relationships
Family	Friends	Justice	Ethics
Truth	Dependability	Sincerity	Spirituality

Use the list as a guide. Feel free to combine or modify them or come up with a value that's entirely different, but right for you.

In my case, I started with the value words *Trust* and *Respect*. Then I combined them into a single value for me: *Mutual Respect and Trust.*

Define the Value in a Sentence or Two

This is where you personalize your values and define what they mean to you. A fact of human existence is that different people can use the same word, but mean very different things. You want to take a sentence or two to define what your values mean to you. All values are personal, even if we use the same words other people use. Here's an example.

I defined *Mutual Respect and Trust* with the following sentence: "I will lead with respect and trust in all my interactions and will look to build trust through my personal character."

Describe the Behaviors That Support the Value

The next step is to put flesh on your value statement. Describe the behaviors that act out your values. Here are the behaviors I need to do to live out my value of *Mutual Respect and Trust:*

» I will tell the truth, no matter the circumstances.
» I will listen first for understanding before attempting to be understood.
» I will actively seek out feedback on how I am perceived as a leader.
» I will treat everyone with respect. Nobody is better than anybody else.

Once you have defined your values and identified the behaviors that demonstrate them, your challenge is to put this to work in your life. Ask yourself: "What can I do every day to make my values visible?"

One behavior I chose was extremely important to my success as the senior leader of manufacturing operations over the years. There were hundreds of people in those manufacturing plants, and I truly valued each of their opinions and thoughts on how it was going in their area of responsibility. So the first thing I did every single morning and before I left every night was to take a walk through the entire manufacturing operation, to touch base with as many people as possible, and see how they're doing.

Walking the plant floor twice every day and stopping to have conversations with everyone was a way for me to live out my value of *Mutual Respect and Trust* and truly stay in tune with the pulse of the organization. It also helped create the culture that we wanted to have in the company, as I wanted all leaders to value the input of every employee.

Walking the plant floor twice every day became a habit for me. When I first decided that the behavior was important, I had to schedule it so I was sure to do it. After a while I walked the floor at the start and end of every day without having to think about whether to do it or not.

Defining the Key Values for Your Team

Just like personal values, organization values are the enduring beliefs that guide employees' choices and actions in the workplace. The values will determine how people behave on a daily basis as they pursue the organization's purpose. It's "the way we do things around here."

Legendary McKinsey leader Marvin Bowers gets credit for that line; he used it to provide a definition of culture. You can think of culture as your organization's values. You can also think of it as the most important part of your work as a leader.

Years ago, consultant Chris Edmonds told me that, as the president of the Banta Catalog Group, I should be spending 75 percent of my time on culture. I thought he was crazy.

We were a publicly traded company where you live and die by your quarterly financial results. So I thought I should spend the vast majority of my time poring over financial statements, operational metrics, labor management, budgets, and the like. In doing so, I thought I was driving improvement by pushing everyone toward our goals.

It took a little while, but I came to realize that if I shifted the focus to creating a culture that allowed for all people to bring their very best (their brains) to work on a daily basis, we would not have to worry about the results. The results would be the applause for doing all the right things on building the culture and developing leaders to drive that culture.

It turned out that the change was good for results, too. Employee engagement improved by 20 percent within six months, and retention went up by 17 percent. And the big thing I was worried about, profit, increased by 36 percent.

That was proof enough for me. From then on I let the financial results be the scoreboard, not the focus. I concentrated on building an environment where people are respected for the great work they do and allowed to be in control of their work and the improvement they drive. When I did that, the results took care of themselves.

Now when I work with clients, I spend more time on values than on any other piece of the foundation. The values of an organization define its culture. The primary job of a servant leader is to concentrate on creating a purpose-driven, values-based culture. Everything you do should be a model of the values. Here are some things I've learned are important.

Your actions will always outweigh your words. You need to model the values all day, every day. But your actions won't do the job by themselves.

If you rely on your actions to demonstrate the values, you put the members of your team in the position of having to figure out exactly what you expect. Some of them will get it wrong and some will get it right. But when you combine example with explicit messages, you make it easier for everyone to understand what's important.

So reference the values when you use them to guide decision-making. Talk about them when you use them to help you choose how to act.

Many organizations with strong cultures require every team member to memorize the purpose and values of the organization. Randomly ask people to recite them in meetings. Start every meeting by celebrating success and asking team members to tell about situations where the values have been lived out.

You'll find lots more ideas in the packet that goes with this chapter. The important point is that creating and maintaining a values-based, purpose-driven culture is your primary job as a leader.

Getting the values and behaviors clarified is just the beginning. Too many organizations view this as a project to get done so they can publish the values on their website and hang them in the lobby. Then they go back to business as usual. It is relatively easy to establish values; it is *extremely hard* to model and live them every day.

Your purpose describes why you are here. Your values describe how you should act. The third part of Building the Foundation is vision. Vision is the lens that helps you concentrate your efforts. That's what we'll discuss in the next chapter.

THE POWER OF VISION

As Jesus walked beside the Sea of Galilee, he saw Simon and his brother Andrew casting a net into the lake, for they were fishermen. "Come, follow me," Jesus said, "and I will send you out to fish for people." At once they left their nets and followed him.
~ Mark 1: 16–18 (NIV)

Before Jesus came along, Simon and Andrew probably had a fairly simple vision for their life. They were subsistence fishermen and that's what they most likely expected to be for the rest of their lives. Jesus expanded their vision.

Jesus was a carpenter, but He didn't call the brothers to be carpenters. Instead, He offered them a vision of the future in their own language. That vision was so powerful that ultimately both would be crucified for their faith. Before that, they would use their particular strengths to do something powerful and world-changing. They would fish for people.

That's what Jesus wants from us today. He doesn't ask us to be "another Jesus." Instead He asks Ron to use his gifts as the CEO of a company and Consuelo to use her gifts as a project manager and you and me to use our gifts in our lives to align with God's calling and to have an impact on others.

Our challenge is to discern and sharpen a vision that grows from our purpose and aligns with God's will for us. That's what this chapter is about.

WHAT'S A VISION?

There are many definitions of *vision*. My favorite is from Jesse Lyn Stoner, co-author with Ken Blanchard of *Full Steam Ahead! Unleash the Power of Vision in Your Work & Life*. Here's how she puts it: "A vision is a clearly articulated, results-oriented picture of a future you intend to create. It is a dream with direction."

Vision answers the question, "What do we want to create?" whereas your purpose is more general and more permanent: *Live a significant and well-balanced life to the Glory of God.* It can remain unchanged forever.

A vacation is like your vision. It grows out of your purpose, but visions change with time.

Let's say that you want to take a vacation trip to San Antonio, Texas, this year. You'll get pretty specific about what you want to do there. Your list of things to do might include visiting the Alamo, spending some time on the River Walk, eating in some of the area's German restaurants, or attending the San Antonio Fiesta.

Of course, you will plan the trip. You'll pick the time of year when you want to go, make your travel plans and reservations, and leave some time for surprises. You may decide to read up on a little of the area's history or plan for a tour to give you more ideas once you're in town.

Your purpose is *to live a significant and well-balanced life to the Glory of God.* That won't change. You value balance, so a behavior is *Take regular vacations.* That will be true every year. But your vacation in San Antonio is the vision for this year, clearly articulated and results-oriented. Those are the kinds of visions that have helped Dan Malmstrom have a successful career.

Today, Dan is the president and founder of Northpoint Professionals. Before that he was a top salesperson for IBM, a member of the top executive team at Great Plains Software, the co-founder of BeAtHome (one of the earliest home automation companies), and president and chief executive officer of Douglas Scientific. He was also involved in the transformation of Battle Lake, Minnesota. That story is an excellent example of the power of vision.

Battle Lake is a small town about two and a half hours northwest of Minneapolis. Dan has a home there, and in 2008 it looked like a lot of other small towns across the country. The downtown was home to an increasing number of empty storefronts. The tourism that fed the town business seemed to be going away. Enrollment in the local schools was declining, and so were test scores.

Residents began working on the problems in 2008. In 2009 they drafted a 100-page vision statement describing Battle Lake the way they imagined it could be. It was very ambitious.

They imagined restoring the downtown and the city parks and streets. They imagined revitalizing the tourism business and the schools. Those were big, complex, and interacting objectives; but by 2014 they were realities.

Traffic flow was improved and local streets had been updated with "gorgeous artistic touches." The area had the highest visitor count in more than twenty years, and the downtown businesses, including five new ones, had their best summer ever. The schools went from mediocre and declining to earning a National Blue Ribbon School award and having the top test scores in the region.

This isn't magic. It took a lot of coordinated hard work by a lot of people to change Battle Lake. But it wouldn't have happened without the power of vision.

WHY VISION IS IMPORTANT

Vision creates clarity. Vision answers the question, "What do I want to create?" Another way to ask that question is "What kind of progress do I want to make?" In his great book, *The 7 Habits of Highly Effective People*, Stephen R. Covey called it beginning with the end in mind. When you can do that, you can make wise choices about planning your days.

Vision creates energy. We get energy from making progress, and vision gives you a way to assess that. Knowing where you're going creates a can-do attitude.

Vision creates focus. You wake up every day knowing where you want to go. In organizations that are led by a shared vision, everyone is focused and knows where they're going.

Vision creates accountability. Think about Battle Lake. Some people were working on improving the streets, and others were working on improving the school district. Still others were working on bringing more tourists to the area and more businesses to downtown. They were all accountable to each other because they shared the vision.

High-performing servant leaders develop a vision for all aspects of their life. That happens in two steps. First you define your key responsibility areas (KRAs).

Define Your Key Responsibility Areas and Build Your Vision

You may be thinking, "Why do I have to define key responsibility areas? Why can't I just get right to the vision part?"

Defining the key responsibility areas first gives you the opportunity to assess your whole life and make sure you're considering everything. Also, knowing your key responsibility areas makes it easier to see how your visions in different areas can work together.

Different people come up with different lists of key responsibility areas. Here's my list:

- » Personal
- » Family
- » Career
- » Community

A friend of mine has a different list:

- » Relationships
- » Financial
- » Physical

» Mental
» Spiritual

There are no wrong answers here. You can use those or look at other ideas in the Help Packet or come up with your own list from scratch. Take the time to give this prayerful consideration.

Now prioritize your KRAs. Which one is most important right now?

SET A VISION AND GOALS FOR EACH KEY RESPONSIBILITY AREA

Knowing your key responsibility areas is important, but it won't help you take specific actions unless you have a vision of the preferred future, and then define goals for each Area for the next year. Your goals define the specific way you want to make progress in that KRA.

In 2015, one aspect of my vision for my career was to create ways to spread the movement of Triune Leadership Services' Model of Servant Leadership, beyond the borders of Minnesota. So I set goals to write a book about it and start to develop online training options for people all over the world.

Define one or, at most, two goals for each KRA. Even if you limit yourself to only one goal each, you will probably have more than three or four goals total. That's more than most people can keep in mind at once, so make a list. As the saying goes, "The palest ink is more powerful than the strongest memory."

There's another reason to make a list. It helps you review your vision and goals frequently.

REVIEW YOUR VISION AND GOALS

Your vision and your goals will change over time. You will achieve some of your goals and move on. Life changes, such as having a child or contracting a severe illness, will change your priorities. That's why it's important to review your vision.

Every year, I imagine what I want to create in each KRA in my life. Then I look at the current reality of each and assess the gap between current reality and what I want to create. That helps me outline my strategy and goals for the upcoming year to make my vision for each area a reality.

That's what works for me. Other people do things differently. One friend of mine has two annual reviews. At mid-year he reviews his business and financial goals. He makes his personal and spiritual goals the subject of prayer and meditation during Advent.

Many studies of goal setting agree that setting goals can help us concentrate on the important things and achieve more. That's where your list of goals can help you stay on track and keep you moving toward success.

The truth is that we human beings are easily distracted. We love to go chasing after shiny new ideas. The urgent often drives out the important in our lives, too. The result is that we often lose sight of our important goals. Your list will pull your attention back to what's important, if you take the time to review it.

Review the list every week or every day. Make your vision part of your prayer life. Your vision will create clarity, energy and focus for you. If you're a leader in an organization, your organizational vision will do those things, too.

CREATE YOUR ORGANIZATIONAL VISION

Vision establishes leadership. It doesn't matter if you're leading a company, like Ron, or a project team, like Consuelo or a volunteer group; vision creates leadership because vision sets the direction for the group.

Without a shared vision, an organization can just keep doing what it has always done, and before they know it they become obsolete. When is the last time you heard of someone signing up for a paid AOL email account, or standing in line to buy a Blackberry, or walking down the street listening to a Walkman? Companies without vision are risking their future.

Things are different for companies with a vision. The vision channels individual efforts to a common goal, and that can yield spectacular results.

When Dan Malmstrom joined Great Plains Software in 1987, they were the only software company in North Dakota. The company couldn't get a loan from the banks because those banks were used to investing in grain bins and farmland. They had never made a loan to what Dan calls "a bunch of kids writing software."

The executive team went off and developed a detailed ten-year vision for the company. The end they imagined was to sell the company to Microsoft. For the only software company in North Dakota to imagine that was incredible, but with vision to guide them they made it happen. In 2000, Microsoft bought Great Plains Software for $1.1 billion. The Great Plains experience is a good example of the power of organizational vision.

Envisioning a preferred future and developing an organizational vision ranks at the top of the most important work of senior leaders. It should not be delegated to anyone else.

It may be helpful to have a professional facilitator run the meetings so all of the leadership team can concentrate on the issues. There will almost always be more than one meeting.

To maximize focus, I like to conduct these vision meetings offsite and away from distractions. In advance of the offsite meeting, have each senior leader participant do some pre-work that requires them to think about their preferred future. Have them document their personal vision for each of the key responsibility areas (KRAs) of the organization. Answer the following questions about each KRA.

» What is new?
» What has been discontinued?
» What things have been strengthened?
» What shortcomings have been addressed?

Here are some things that would be KRAs for most organizations. Your organization's list may be slightly different.

» Culture
» Value proposition
» Financial performance
» Market
» Operations performance

» Talent/succession
» Leadership development

Have someone collect and consolidate everyone's answers so that these individual best thoughts about the future can be collectively discussed when the group is together.

As a facilitator, I like to kick off the vision meeting with a review of the organization's purpose and values because the vision needs to reflect those. Then have leadership team members share their personal vision of the organization. After everyone has a chance to share their top priorities and what they are most passionate about when thinking about their preferred future, start building an aligned vision. Capture and discuss the common themes for each KRA and build consensus around the vision of the organization.

This will normally take a number of iterations. It is sometimes beneficial to run the vision past other stakeholders who were not involved in the details, just to hear their reaction and get their feedback. Take that feedback into consideration as you finalize the vision.

It is then important to examine the current reality for each KRA. Current reality is where you are today. As Jesse Lyn Stoner says, "people that focus only on their vision have their heads in the clouds, and likewise people that only focus on current reality have their feet stuck in the mud. Only those that maintain a vision and honestly look at their current situation at the same time can achieve their vision."

By looking at both, you will identify the gap between where you are and where your vision directs the organization. The team can then build strategies, plans, and commitments to bridge the gap for each key responsibility area.

This process will work for any sized team, but you won't learn it by just thinking about it. You have to try it.

Pick one team you are currently leading, or are a part of, that does not currently have a well-defined vision. Pull your team together and discuss what you want to create in the upcoming year in each of your Key Responsibility Areas. Develop a vision for each KRA, as well as a few key goals within each one to move you towards your ideal future.

LEADING JESUS' WAY
TO BUILD THE FOUNDATION

Write down the revelation and make it plain on tablets
so that whoever reads it may run with it.
~ Habakkuk 2:2 (NIV)

Jesus lived His life on purpose, He made daily choices based on His core values, and He understood His vision. Jesus was a servant leader, and His life is the model for our lives as faith-based servant leaders. At the very beginning of His ministry, in the synagogue in Nazareth, Jesus shared an intentional statement of purpose, values, and vision:

The Spirit of the Lord is on me, because he has anointed
me to proclaim good news to the poor. He has sent me
to proclaim freedom for the prisoners and recovery
of sight for the blind, to set the oppressed free, to
proclaim the year of the Lord's favor.
~ Luke 4:18–19 (NIV)

Jesus had purpose. He was the "anointed" or designated activator of God's ultimate intention for the world He created. He knew He was God's Son, that God loved Him, and was proud of Him.

Jesus lived out simple and consistent values. His words and actions recorded for us in the Gospels relay five primary strategies:

» Good news for the poor—Jesus *valued and delivered provision.*
» Release for captives—Jesus *pardoned the guilty.*
» Sight for the blind—Jesus *healed broken bodies, minds, and hearts.*
» Freedom for the oppressed—Jesus *delivered people from the enemy's domination.*
» Proclaiming the year of the Lord's favor—Jesus *announced God's love.*

Jesus had vision. He understood that the outcome of His presence and His work would be a revolution, wherein all of creation would be restored to God's original plan.

That was Jesus' purpose here on Earth. Those were the values that He lived out. That was His vision.

Jesus calls us to servant leadership which He has modeled for us. He does not call us to be "another Jesus." He does call us to use the unique gifts God has given us to align with God's calling and have an impact on others. Jesus' life modeled the servant leadership He calls us to.

Before you begin working with your team, you should prepare yourself to be a model for them. I believe that personal mastery precedes professional mastery. Take the time to develop your own foundation: your purpose, values, and vision. Then you can be a role model for your team as you lead them through the process of developing the team's foundation. Here are some thoughts about doing that well.

Building a foundation and a culture of intention is truly a process and a journey that will never end, but it needs to start somewhere. Building momentum is an important part of the process. One great description of how that process works is the "flywheel" effect that Jim Collins describes in *Good to Great—Why Some Companies Make the Leap... And Others Don't*: "relentlessly pushing a giant heavy flywheel in one direction, turn upon turn, building momentum until a point of breakthrough, and beyond." In other words, it won't be quick and it won't be easy. Many times you and your team members will wonder if all the effort is worth it. That's natural. Remember that it *will* be worth the effort and time. Here are some things I've learned that make the process as effective as possible.

» Go offsite with your leadership team for this work. If you can combine it with some team-building work, even better!
» Frame-up the work in advance, letting the team know what they will be working on, as well as the importance of the work.
» Utilize a facilitator to help drive the process so that everyone can fully participate in the development of the Foundation.

Those are basic guidelines. Here's an agenda I've learned will be effective when you're starting the journey to build the foundation:

Develop and share the personal purpose/values/vision of the team members. This will build team chemistry as members of the team gain an understanding of the foundation of each of their peers.

Organization purpose is next. Establish what you do, for whom you do it, and, most importantly, why. Break your team into smaller groups so each comes up with what they feel is an authentic purpose statement for the organization. Then pull the groups together, and build from the ideas that have been generated to come to a final purpose statement.

Determine the values and behaviors necessary to effectively carry out the purpose of the organization. Limit yourself to the four or five most important values. Develop definitions that further clarify what each value means. Then establish specific behaviors behind each value to provide guidance for the organization on how to carry out that value.

Organization vision work is usually a process and journey within itself. I recommend setting aside specific time for this, once the purpose and values have been established. Because the vision may change, review your vision on a regular basis, either annually or bi-annually, to keep the vision updated with current reality.

The process of building foundation and driving culture is a never-ending journey. Once you build momentum, it's hard to slow down, as it becomes the focus of attention for employees and all stakeholders in a positive way. Team members will be cheering on team members, yours will become the desired place to work, customers will want to work with you, and your performance will improve.

Building the foundation is, well, the foundation for servant leadership. The foundation supports everything else. There's a lot of work in this section, and it should be done carefully and prayerfully. Don't rush through it. When you're ready, go to the next chapter and learn how to build the energy that will make your team an exciting and productive group to be a part of.

BUILD ENERGY

INTRODUCTION

The next key task for a servant leader is to build energy. You serve the organization by creating an environment where people are energized and actively engaged in the pursuit of the organization's purpose and vision.

People do not automatically follow and get charged up by a worthy cause. But they will follow passionate leaders who lead with energy and promote values and a vision that they believe in.

Your team will not show more energy and passion than you do. As Lee Iacocca said, "The speed of the leader is the speed of the team." You set the pace and model the way.

Your energy and passion will be contagious. Think about the impact that passionate, worthy leaders such as Martin Luther King Jr. and Abraham Lincoln had on our country. These were individuals people wanted to follow, thanks to their own passion and energy that they had around a worthy cause.

You don't need to look to history for examples, though. Look around you. Look at the leaders you know in your life. I think you'll find that almost all of them set the pace, as well as the example, for their teams.

The six key elements of building energy within a team are:

» Maintain your own energy
» Clarify and communicate the foundation (purpose/values/vision)
» Connect people and their roles to the foundation

» Set up boundaries and put people in control of the goal
» Recognize people and offer gratitude
» Invest in the development of people

We will delve into each of these key areas of building energy in this section of the book. But before you move on, take a few moments to do this exercise.

Think of a leader you know who has a significant amount of energy around a specific purpose. It will probably be one of the leaders you identified a couple of minutes ago. What are some ways this leader builds energy within the team to effectively advance the purpose?

When you're ready, turn the page and we'll dive into maintaining your own energy.

MAINTAIN YOUR OWN ENERGY

Do you not know?
Have you not heard?
The Lord is the everlasting God,
the Creator of the ends of the earth
He will not grow tired or weary,
and his understanding no one can fathom.
He gives strength to the weary
and increases the power of the weak.
Even youths grow tired and weary,
and young men stumble and fall;
but those who hope in the Lord
will renew their strength.
They will soar on wings like eagles;
they will run and not grow weary,
they will walk and not be faint.
— Isaiah 40: 28–31 (NIV)

As a leader, I always knew it was up to me to set the pace for the energy within the team. If I was feeling down, I knew it would rub off on the team, and they would be down as well. But if I showed up with a great deal of energy and enthusiasm, it would be infectious.

I also realized that if I relied on myself for this it would be like riding a roller coaster. Many things could impact my mood and energy if I allowed it. I had to rely on these verses in Isaiah 40. When I relied on the Lord each day to renew my strength and provide never ending energy, I would soar on wings like eagles and not become weary, and that would have a positive impact on people around me.

It's funny, but I discovered that I need to rely on those verses to maintain the discipline to do all the little things that help me maintain my energy. If you want to maintain the energy you need to lead well, you have to make dozens of choices every day to do the things that build your personal energy.

I'm a big sports fan, and one of my favorite quotes about energy is this classic from legendary football coach Vince Lombardi: "Fatigue makes cowards of us all."

That might be okay, if it was the whole story. But when we're tired, we're not just more likely to be cowardly; we're also more likely to be irritable, less likely to be effective, and far less likely to be disciplined.

When I was overtired, I was less likely to take the time to walk the plant floor at the beginning and end of the day. When I got out of my routine and tired, I was less likely to do all the things that I knew I should do. It's probably that way for you, too. And the insidious thing is that it doesn't happen all at once.

Just recently, I overloaded my schedule to the point that I missed the necessary sleep, exercise, and proper nutrition that I have found important in maintaining my well-being. This led to my being rundown. I caught a cold, and my energy level dropped to the point where I wasn't doing right by my family or my clients. The only solution was to get back on track and start doing things right again.

THE BODY-MIND-SPIRIT MIRACLE

We human beings are the crowning miracle of God's creation. We are an amazing system made up of three parts: our body, our mind, and our spirit. In the last couple of decades, scientists and other researchers have been discovering just what a marvel that system is.

Each part of the system affects the other parts. That means that when one part is down, it will affect other parts. But it also means that when one part is down, we can affect it through the other parts. We Christians have a real advantage here because of our spiritual component.

Through our study of scripture and through prayer, we can begin to deal with problems in the body and in the mind. When your energy begins to run down, you can remember the verses from Isaiah above. You can pray for guidance for strength. You can rely on the Lord for help.

Maintaining your own energy can give you powerful results. Writing in the *Harvard Business Review*, Tony Schwartz and Catherine McCarthy reported on the results of an "energy renewal" program they conducted at a major bank. Here's part of what they found.

> Sixty-eight percent reported that it had a positive impact on their relationships with clients and customers. Seventy-one percent said that it had a noticeable or substantial positive impact on their productivity and performance.

If you maintain your energy, you can be the kind of leader God wants you to be. You will be able to do the things that make you an effective servant leader. You will be able to do the little things every day that make servant leaders effective. Let's start by thinking about caring for your body.

BODY

Do you not know that your bodies are temples of the Holy Spirit, who is in you, whom you have received from God? You are not your own; you were bought at a price. Therefore honor God with your bodies.
—1 Corinthians 6:19–20 (NIV)

Get your sleep. Not getting enough sleep makes you more stressed and more anxious and in general affects your mind. Sleep deprivation makes it hard to feel and stay positive, hard to concentrate, and hard to be creative. When you're tired, your working memory shrinks so you have limited ability to concentrate, learn, listen, and solve problems. Finding ways to improve your sleep will enhance your ability to effectively lead and serve others.

Most of us need a *minimum* of seven hours' sleep a night, and most of us will be better with eight. But the amount of sleep isn't the only concern; you want as much *good quality* sleep as possible.

Sleep experts tell us that we're more likely to get good quality sleep if we go to sleep and wake up at the same times every day. They recommend a cool (not cold) dark room and a good mattress. Some people like to use a white noise generator or a fan to block out distracting noises.

Get your exercise. Your body is the engine for high performance, so you need to keep it functional and in good shape. Being fit greatly affects your happiness in life. Make it a habit to exercise regularly, that is, several times a week.

Regular exercise doesn't necessarily mean a rigorous weight training program or running triathlons. If that's for you, great; but most people will choose a less demanding fitness program. Make sure that you cover the three main areas of fitness, though. Do some strength training, especially for those muscles in your torso that affect your posture and breathing. Many of these exercises don't require any equipment. Do some stretching for flexibility. Lots of people like yoga for this. And do some cardiovascular exercise, the things that get your heart rate up for twenty minutes or so. There are lots of options, from real and stationary bicycles, stair climbers, and cross-training machines, through jogging and brisk walking.

Eat Healthy. What you eat can impact how you feel overall and what kind of energy level you have throughout each day. What you eat affects how your brain and mind work. When your body is functioning well, it feeds your brain, and you will find it easier to stay positive. If you want to be a high performer, watch what you eat.

Others have come up with a lot of rules that can help you. I like the one that says "Don't eat anything that your great grandmother wouldn't recognize." Those sayings are fun and helpful, but I've found that most people know what "eating healthy" means. For most of us it means eating relatively simple foods in reasonable portions.

Pay attention to how eating affects your energy. You'll discover that some foods seem to suck energy out of you as your body uses energy to digest them. So don't eat those before a meeting. Learn what works for you: how often and how much you should eat.

MIND AND EMOTIONS

We know that we are all unique creatures because God made each of us special and different from everyone else. But we've also learned that there are some ways in which most of us are the same. God gave most of us the same basic internal wiring. You will do better if you use that wiring instead of trying to change it. Here are some ways to do that.

Do the hard stuff when your brain is fresh. Schedule difficult tasks and hard thinking for when your brain is full of energy. For most of us, that's the early part of the day. Your brain is like a muscle that tires as the day goes on.

Don't multi-task. Many research studies have shown that multi-tasking degrades performance.

Use the body's natural rhythms. Your body has a natural cycle of 90 to 120 minutes during which you move from a high energy state to a lower energy state. As you come to the end of the cycle, you may start yawning and have difficulty concentrating. That's the signal that it's time to take a break.

Take breaks. Short breaks rekindle your energy for productive work. What's a break? It's something different. Leave your work station and go talk to a colleague. Take a walk. Answer emails. Clean up your workspace. It doesn't matter what you do, as long as it's different from what you were doing when you started yawning.

Don't simply take a few minutes off here and there. Take longer breaks, too. Take time off on the weekends to do something that has nothing to do with work. Take a vacation—a real one where you're not checking email all the time.

Give thanks! Be thankful for all your blessings. Being thankful will fulfill your soul and lead to good health and a positive outlook on life.

Cultivate relationships. God made us to be social beings. We're at our happiest and most effective when we're connected to friends and family. In our hustle-bustle, high-tech world, it's easy to fall into the mistaken belief that Facebook friends are enough. Your family and friends are important. Give them the time they deserve.

SPIRIT

If there is a secret sauce for the faith-based servant leader, this is it. If we had to rely on ourselves, we could get overwhelmed. But we can lean on God, who makes all things possible.

Pray often. We often have more on our plate than we can handle. I think God intends it that way, so that we know we need to rely on Him. Take everything to God in prayer. Maintain consistent conversation with your Father, leaning on Him for health, guidance, wisdom, comfort, and peace.

Spend time in devotion/reflection. We all have a calling in our life from God. We have been gifted with talents and passions that God wants us to use to advance His Kingdom. Spending daily time with God studying scripture and reflecting on what your priorities should be that day will enhance your effectiveness.

Love God/love your neighbor. Good health and a positive life can resonate from your heart. Staying focused on this command from God will keep you focused on what is really important in life and ensure that you are taking care of your self to ensure that you can love God and your neighbors.

Maintaining your personal energy will make you a more effective faith-based servant leader. Your personal energy sets the example for your team members and enables you to generate energy in your team, starting with your communication of the foundation.

COMMUNICATE THE FOUNDATION

*Blessed rather are those who hear
the word of God and obey it.*
—Luke 11:28 (NIV)

In this verse Jesus turns a compliment into a lesson. He has been talking with people and sharing one teaching story after another. A woman in the crowd calls out, "Blessed be the mother who gave you birth and nursed you."

Jesus seizes the opportunity to share His message and make an important point. He does that over and over throughout the gospels. Whatever situation He is in, Jesus seizes the opportunity to share His message. You have the same challenge as a servant leader.

I had lots of great conversations when I took my walks around the plant every day. Those walks also presented opportunities to share our purpose, values, and vision in the flow of conversation.

In any manufacturing organization I have ever led, one of our values was always *employee well being*, and a key part of that value was *safety and housekeeping*. I wanted to communicate that by setting the example.

Whenever I was out in the manufacturing area I would make it a point to pick up any debris that was on the floor and discard it. A printing plant can get really messy (and dangerous) if people don't stay on top of safety and housekeeping.

I also took every opportunity to compliment equipment operators, material handlers, and others when their workspace was spotless. Our vision was to have a "medical clean room" type of mentality that would blow our customers away when they were in our printing facilities.

But blowing customers away wasn't the most important thing. *Employee well being* was the most important part. If I communicated that by word and deed, our people would go home safely at night.

I discovered that three benefits grew out of my constant communication. The people I talked with benefited by hearing the foundation. It reinforced their knowledge of what was important. Talking about the foundation helped make it a part of me, too. And discussing the foundation with other men and women also created a bond of accountability between us.

Research supports this. Harvard professor John Kotter studied the work patterns of general managers in US companies. He thought he would discover that the most effective general managers were the ones with tightly controlled schedules. Instead, he found that the most effective ones were those who used lots of informal conversations to learn from others and share their message of what was important.

That doesn't mean that planning your day isn't important. In fact, a little bit of planning will help you communicate the foundation more effectively. Here's how it works for me.

Every morning I ask myself how I will *Glorify God by helping leaders to lead at a higher level, to enable them to achieve their God-given potential* in the day ahead. Thinking about how I am going to advance that purpose each morning gives me energy. At the end of the day, I review how I did by asking myself what I did that day to advance my purpose.

The same holds true for my values and my vision. Reciting them to myself each morning gives me energy to step into them and model them throughout the day.

Professionally, it's also extremely important to communicate your foundation at every possible opportunity. When the company purpose, values, and vision are first formalized, I like to make a big deal of it at all-employee meetings.

I share with people that, even though I am the president, the new boss in the organization is our purpose, values, and vision. This foundation is the boss. Everyone's first responsibility is to hold me as the senior leader, responsible for modeling these values and making decisions in line with our purpose and vision.

That's great. After you make a big deal of the Foundation at an all-employee meeting, everyone is excited and ready to get after it. But that energy dies out pretty quickly if you don't do something to keep the fire burning.

It's just like feeding a campfire. If you're not feeding it constantly, it's going to die down. If you're not feeding the culture you want, it's going to die down.

Many of my clients require all leaders to have their purpose and values memorized. Review them at every meeting.

The bottom line is that you have to take advantage of every opportunity to keep the fire burning, to refresh everyone's understanding of the foundation. Two keys are memorizing purpose and values and constantly telling stories about people who live them out.

Ritz-Carlton is known for creating a legendary customer experience. They've been doing it for decades, and part of their secret is exactly what we've been talking about. Ritz-Carlton requires everyone who works there to understand their Credo, Motto, and the Three Steps of Service. They incorporate discussion of those three (their version of the foundation) into their daily meetings that begin each shift.

The leaders in those daily meetings also ask team members to share stories that illustrate someone else's living out the Ritz-Carlton values. The daily meetings, discussion of their foundation, and storytelling help make sure that everyone in the organization knows what's expected.

That's how Ritz-Carlton does it. Here are some things that have worked for me.

» Start each meeting by discussing how the group has advanced the purpose since the last meeting.
» Share stories and celebrate when people have modeled the behaviors you are looking for within the culture.

» Take decisive action with team members who consistently do not model the expected behaviors of the organization.
» Be intentional about finding out how team members think you're modeling the values, and correct your behavior based on their feedback.
» Spend at least 50 percent of your leadership time and effort focusing on people and driving the culture you want.

EXERCISE

Before you move on to the next chapter, work the following exercises.

» Memorize your personal and organization foundations.

» Develop two daily habits that will help you keep your personal and organizational fires burning.

» Survey your team to determine how well they understand the organization's purpose, values, and vision. Then work with the team and develop three practices that will help keep the foundation of the organization at the forefront of everyone's mind.

CONNECT PEOPLE AND THEIR ROLES TO THE FOUNDATION

For God so loved the world that he gave his one and only Son, that whoever believes in him shall not perish but have eternal life.
— John 3:16 (NIV)

That's a powerful purpose, and Jesus was the Son of God. But even Jesus needed to reach out to His Father in prayer to understand how important His work was. If He didn't go to the cross, the mission would not be completed. If He didn't show up to complete His work, all would be lost.

If Jesus needed constant prayer to achieve His mission, how much more do we need that prayer, that connection of our work to our purpose and our organization's purpose? To be an effective servant leader, you must help people connect their roles to the accomplishment of the purpose.

People need to know that if they don't show up, the mission will not be accomplished. It is your responsibility to help them make that connection.

Once the foundation is set and well communicated, servant leaders build energy by constantly reminding people why their work is critical and that, without them and their work, the vision will not become real.

THIS WON'T HAPPEN AUTOMATICALLY

You cannot assume that people will automatically find alignment with the purpose of the organization. Some people will make the connection, but many will not.

It is very easy for heart surgeons to connect what they are doing to the purpose of the hospital. It's easy for them to understand how important their work is. They are clearly saving lives and helping people. But what about other people working in the same hospital?

The people who clean the rooms, the ones who purchase supplies, and the person at the front desk may not see the way their work connects to the hospital's purpose. That's a challenge. Here are some things I have found to be effective in helping employees connect to the organization's purpose and realize the importance of their work.

WAYS TO HELP PEOPLE CONNECT THEIR WORK TO THE PURPOSE, VALUES, AND VISION

New-employee orientation programs should clearly articulate the organization's purpose, values, and vision. But don't stop there. Illustrate how the work that the employee will be doing relates to the achievement of the purpose.

Bring in customers to speak at all-employee meetings to let employees know how critical they are to the customers' success. Videotape interviews with customers in which they tell your people the difference their work makes in the customer's life and work.

My company printed all the invoices for one of the monster cell-phone companies. We brought in a couple of their executives to talk to our people. They told our people that their company wouldn't be as successful as they were without the printing support our people gave them.

Tell the stories of some of your customers' customers to show the importance of the entire supply chain and how what is being done makes a big difference in society. Here's an example from when I was president of a catalog company.

The people who worked in our plants were doing pretty mundane work eight, ten, or twelve hours a day. They didn't see the catalogs that were our product. And it was hard for them to imagine all the great things that catalog could be part of.

So we went out and asked one of our customers, a wine merchant, if they could help us to connect our people to the importance of the work that they're doing. And they said, "Absolutely. That would be wonderful."

We interviewed them and they talked about the importance of how critical it was that our people printed the catalog properly, that they got it trimmed and stitched, and got it mailed on time. That was great, but we took it one step further.

We went out to one of their customers who had bought wine through the catalog and served it at their wedding reception. We videotaped them having this one single greatest time of their life, drinking the wine they bought through the catalog. Then our customer came back on the video and said, "If you hadn't done your job, this couple, our customer, would not have had this phenomenal time at their wedding. You are making these moments possible."

Take your employees out to a customer's site or organization to see the impact of their work first hand. My wife worked for a high-end cabinet shop that takes its employees on an annual bus tour to the homes of people who have installed their cabinetry. It gives employees the opportunity to hear from the customers and see what amazing living spaces they are creating.

I was able to go on a couple of those bus tours with them. It was inspiring to see those employees when customers were telling them what amazing work they did and thanking them for it. And they got to see the phenomenal cabinetry that they had built installed in these multimillion-dollar homes. The last time they had seen those cabinets they were just a bunch of wood pieces leaving the shop.

Talk about how the work that employees are doing is achieving the purpose of the organization. Relate all decisions and actions to how it is advancing the purpose and values.

Allow employees to see and experience other areas of the organization though plant tours, cross-training, job shadowing, etc.

Servant leaders realize that when people understand how worthwhile their work is, and can connect that work to the achievement of the organization's purpose, they are passionate about their work! Passion in the workplace is infectious and builds energy. Customers want to be associated with people who have a passion for their work. Southwest Airlines and Ritz Carlton are both great examples of this, but your organization can be a great example, too.

EXERCISE

» Reflect on how your personal purpose is making a difference in the world. What specifically is happening due to your daily efforts of advancing your personal purpose?

» Work with your team to develop three new ways that you could help connect the dots for your employees to help them understand the difference they are making by doing their jobs every day.

» What are you doing as a leader to ensure that your people know how important their work is to the achievement of the purpose?

SET UP BOUNDARIES AND PUT PEOPLE IN CONTROL OF THE GOAL

His master replied, "Well done, good and faithful servant! You have been faithful with a few things; I will put you in charge of many things. Come and share your master's happiness!"
— Matthew 25:21 (NIV)

I was blessed to have the opportunity to lead a significant number of people at an early age. I was a plant manager of a printing plant with about 300 operations employees in Milwaukee at the age of 26. Two years later, I was a vice-president/general manager of a printing plant in Long Prairie, Minnesota, with about 400 employees. I was probably not qualified for those roles at that age, but I was successful because I understood the importance of setting up boundaries and putting people in control of their own destiny.

I knew without a doubt that all the people in these operations knew far more than I about how to do their job. So I set the expectations of where we wanted to be, and then allowed them to do their job and generate ideas on how to improve. When people showed the capacity to excel, I gave them more responsibility. My job was to tell them how much I appreciated their great work!

ASSESS PASSION AND COMPETENCE

It's your job to assess the passion and competence of your people and then lead them accordingly. It is important in building energy to allow people to do what they do best, with as much freedom and control as possible.

The assessment process is critical. You have to determine their real competence and their willingness to pitch in to do the job before you make decisions about how to supervise.

When people are new to an organization or profession they are probably going to need a lot of direction from you. They want specific guidance from you about what to do and when and how to do it. When you provide the guidance, they will be learning and that will generate energy.

But as people get more proficient in their work, all that guidance will drain energy from them. Once they know how to do the work, they are closest to the action and are familiar with what is coming at them. They need the authority to make calls and create as necessary. Giving them freedom and control will build their energy.

BUILD ENERGY IN TWO STEPS

You build energy in two steps. First, you set boundaries for people, based on their level of competence and their willingness to pitch in and do the job. Then you allow them to think, act, and react on their own within those boundaries.

I'm a sports fan, and I like to use the example of a football coach and his running back. The coach has trained the running back in practice, and has made the expectations clear. The running back is to take the ball and run down to the end zone, while staying within the two sidelines (the boundaries). Once the running back is on the field and the play starts, the coach's work is over. Then it's up to the running back to make all the course corrections necessary to deliver on the coach's expectations.

DON'T TRY TO DO IT ALL

When I'm working as an executive coach, I can usually spot problems in this area with leaders. When my client feels totally overwhelmed on the job because they have to make all the decisions, it's a sign that they're trying to do it all themselves.

Sometimes that happens because the executive is afraid that if he or she lets others take some control, the work won't get done as well. That may be true. But if you're the leader, your job is to develop leaders throughout the organization who will ensure that all the work gets done as well as possible.

This can be a win for everyone. You can make your life easier and improve performance and morale by setting boundaries and then giving people control of the goal.

You may recognize yourself in that situation; I know I have from time to time. Does everyone seem to come to you for problems to be solved and decisions to be made? If so, you are probably not setting up the boundaries and putting people in control. The higher you go in the organization, the more this is a problem.

THE HIGHER YOU GO, THE FEWER DECISIONS YOU SHOULD MAKE

The higher you go, the less you know about all the day-to-day knowledge about your areas of responsibility. You should be making fewer decisions, not more. Servant leaders recognize this and focus on building their teams' competencies. They tell others, "You decide!"

A great example of this was when I was running a major catalog printing company. I knew we needed faster bindery equipment to compete effectively in a highly competitive marketplace. The company we bought the equipment from had been working on the problem for years, but they hadn't cracked the code.

So we turned the problem over to the people in our operation who knew the most about the bindery operation. Our bindery manager took three of his top equipment operators and two of our best machinists off the floor for three months. They spent that time with the engineers at the equipment manufacturer to try to develop faster equipment.

They developed machinery that was about 20 percent faster than anything on the market at that time. It was breakthrough technology that gave us a big competitive edge. And it would never have happened if we hadn't put people in control of the goal. There were other benefits, too.

The project built a huge amount of energy in the team and throughout the entire organization. It was a great example of how people could use their knowledge to make the company better. It was a win all around.

There's one more benefit of putting people in control of their own destiny. It's much more sustainable than leaving all the decisions to top leaders. It builds energy within the team and allows you to focus on what you do best, in order to maximize your own impact.

Here are some things you can do to help people be in control of the goal.

» Clarify what you expect as outcomes from your team's work, and don't be afraid to consistently raise expectations as capabilities improve.
» Let your people know how critical they are to the success of the team/organization.
» Have a discussion to determine and agree upon each person's level of competence and the amount of your involvement they need for different tasks.
» Clarify their boundaries.
» Allow them to do their work and make decisions without micro-managing them.
» Actively praise them for the great work they are doing.

TAKE A "COACH APPROACH"

Then take a "Coach Approach" to your leadership. Listen intently, acknowledge ideas, ask powerful questions that will promote further discovery, and encourage your team members to reach for their best.

Don't allow people to push decisions up. When they come to you for an answer or specific direction, possible responses might include these:

» What are you thinking about the possibilities?
» What do your instincts tell you?
» Maybe there isn't just one answer.
» My answer might not be right for you.

» This is about you, not about me.
» I have confidence in you. Your solution is best.

Here's a summary of the benefits I have found from using a "Coach Approach":

» Aligns with a culture of servant leadership
» Emphasizes the unique potential of individuals
» Provides structure and process for personal development
» Establishes the focus on the person being coached—not the leader
» Promotes personal discovery and self-responsibility in solving problems
» Fosters the development of high levels of self-confidence and mastery
» *Builds performance!*

EXERCISE

Conduct an informal survey with your team to determine their understanding of their expectations and their satisfaction with your level of involvement in helping them accomplish that goal.

RECOGNIZE AND ENCOURAGE PEOPLE

Therefore encourage one another and build each other up, just as in fact you are doing.
— 1 Thessalonians 5:11 (NIV)

I've had to work at many things in my life, but encouraging people comes naturally. I love recognizing the great work and skills and behavior of other people. I've learned that it's one of the greatest gifts God gave me, because encouragement gives people strength. It's the most powerful thing you can do to get more of the behavior and performance you want.

If you want to build energy in your team, praise people. Encourage them to do more of the good things they do, and they will. Author Michael LeBeouf calls it "The Greatest Management Principle in the World." Jan Carlzon, CEO of Sweden's national airline and author of *Moments of Truth,* says it straight out: "Praise generates energy."

At the core, servant leadership is about thinking first and foremost about the well-being of others. Encouragement is the act of stepping into the lives of people and telling them what they need to hear. As it says in Hebrews 10:24, "And let us consider how we may spur one another on toward love and good deeds."

HOW YOU CAN ENCOURAGE PEOPLE

Getting intentional about encouraging others is one of the most potent things you can do as a servant leader. It builds energy within the team.

You can encourage people in the following ways:

- » *By what you give.* You can encourage others by giving them something you have now.
- » *By what you say.* Be intentional about encouraging others with your communications. Proverbs 16:24 says: "Gracious words are a honeycomb, sweet to the soul and healing to the bones."
- » *By what you do.* You encourage others when you support them and pitch in to help them.
- » *By how you choose to live your life.* Positive behavior in all situations encourages others.

When you encourage others, you give them confidence and build their self-esteem. That sets up a powerful cycle of personal growth, willingness to take risks, and persistence. It enables people to achieve their God-given potential. And it builds energy!

Be an encourager. Seize every opportunity to build up and encourage the people around you. If you take nothing else from this book, please commit yourself to be intentional about encouraging others.

CATCH PEOPLE DOING THINGS RIGHT

Servant leaders understand that one of their most important responsibilities is to catch people doing the right thing and then let them know how much they are appreciated. Too many leaders I've seen concentrate on the negatives, catching people doing things wrong, but if that's all you do, you drain the energy out of the environment.

I don't believe that people come into work each day intending to screw up. I sure don't do that, and I've never met anyone who did. No, they come in to do great work and advance the company's purpose. Our job as servant leaders is to help them do great work and achieve great things. I find that people who have been consistently encouraged

- » Make better teammates,
- » Are more productive,

» Are more creative and willing to take risks to drive improvement,
» Have less fear of failure,
» Feel empowered, and
» Are open to being coached when problems arise.

Here are some tips on how to do a good job of catching people doing things right:

» Recognize both good performance and good behaviors.
» Recognize the small wins as well as the big wins.
» Recognize effort and improvement as well as achievement.
» Put practices in place to make recognition a daily habit.

I used to start every meeting with a celebration of the success stories that team members had seen since our last meeting. Those stories and our daily performance metrics provided plenty of material for me to recognize people.

On my daily walks I also looked for the good work people did, such as employees' keeping a safe, clean, and orderly work space, or pitching in to help others in need. When I caught them doing things like that, I complimented them on being a great teammate.

DEVELOP THE HABIT OF ENCOURAGEMENT

I know that encouraging people comes naturally to me; I do it without thinking too much about it. Encouragement is one of the gifts God gave me. And, as we're told in Romans, "We have different gifts, according to the grace given to each of us." If you don't have the gift of encouragement, you need to develop the habit of encouragement.

One of my favorite examples of a leader making encouragement a daily habit was a senior leader who was a fisherman. He would put six fishing jigs (sans hooks) in his left pocket every morning. Each time he caught someone doing the right thing, he complimented him or her and then moved a jig to his right pocket. His goal was to finish each day with all the jigs in his right pocket.

Another leader used bright yellow cards with the words "'preciate ya!" on them to mimic her Texas accent. Whenever she caught someone doing something right, she handed them one of the cards. Later, at team meetings, she publicly recognized the people who had received cards and asked them to tell the team what they were doing at the time.

These encouragement practices drive a culture of

» Trust,
» Energized employees,
» Confidence,
» High performance,
» Innovation,
» Personal growth, and
» Positive relationships

I know this does not always come naturally for everyone. But I firmly believe that a leader can develop an attitude of gratitude by working at developing the habit of gratitude.

Here are a few ideas for improving your leadership through gratitude. I'm sure you can come up with more.

Make gratitude intentional and routine. Make it a habit. If this doesn't come naturally for you, this will take some effort. You're sure to feel uncomfortable at times. But it's worth it.

Be specific. Don't just tell someone "Great job." Instead, let them know how their specific performance or behavior has made a true difference.

Don't dilute your praise with a but. When you qualify your praise or add a negative, you drain the energy and power right out of it.

When appropriate, make it a big deal and show appreciation publicly. Team meetings are a great place for public recognition. You can have team members recognize each other for good work.

Give handwritten notes of appreciation. Handwritten notes take more effort, and they mean more to the recipient. One leader I know handed them out at meetings. Another one mailed the note to the team member's home, so his or her family could savor the praise, too.

Welcome and appreciate gratitude. Graciously accept gratitude coming your way. Say "Thank you."

At the start of the day, identify someone who needs encouragement. Then make giving that encouragement one of the important things you do that day.

We say that "what gets measured gets done." Some leaders apply this principle to praise and encouragement. They keep track of the number of times each day that they catch people doing something right and how many times they catch someone doing something wrong.

Make no mistake, negative comments are sometimes appropriate. Jack Zenger and Joseph Folkman make that case in a *Harvard Business Review* article titled "The Ideal Praise-to-Criticism Ratio":

> So, while a little negative feedback apparently goes a long way, it is an essential part of the mix. Why is that? First, because of its ability to grab someone's attention. Think of it as a whack on the side of the head. Second, certainly, negative feedback guards against complacency and groupthink. And third, our own research shows, it helps leaders overcome serious weaknesses.

Note that Zenger and Folkman say "a little negative feedback." They go on in the article to analyze what they've learned from studying their database of the 360-degree feedback on more than 50,000 leaders. Their conclusion is straightforward:

> We submit that all leaders should be aware of the ratio of positive and negative comments made by their colleagues in lead-

ership team meetings, and endeavor to move the proportion closer to the ideal of 5.6 to 1.

If you need a target, that's a pretty good one, but don't worry about a specific ratio. Concentrate on increasing the number of times you catch people doing something right, and use specific praise to encourage them.

35 DAYS OF ENCOURAGEMENT

I feel that encouragement is so important that I developed a "35 Days of Encouragement Challenge." It is a tool I provide to clients to help them step into intentional action around building an environment of encouragement to build energy in their organization. You can download it from our website. Here are some comments from people who have taken the challenge.

» What a breath of fresh air. There always seems to be so much negativity in the air, and it's great to see and experience the various examples of encouragement. We all need it.

» A practical way that we seek to verbally encourage people is in restaurants. Waiters and waitresses deal with the public all day long and can be exposed to some pretty demanding and even rude treatment. We try to be the best customers they've had all day! This has led to some remarkable conversations, Gospel interactions, and prayer opportunities. Encouragement. It works!

» Yesterday was such a joy. I had the opportunity to pray with a co-worker and bring her flowers in a moment of great distress.

» Encouraging others is difficult for me. However, I feel so warm when I do encourage someone, seeing and feeling the reaction as you lift them up.

» One thing I taught my sons when they were in high school was to appreciate the cooks and the janitors. The cooks give you an extra scoop and the janitors have the key to the gym. So today I made a point to thank the cook, front door guard, the techs, mailroom people, in others words those behind the scenes.

One big "Aha!" for me is that too often leaders focus only on encouraging those under their leadership. That's great. But don't forget that your peers and boss can use encouragement, too. Besides, sharing encouragement all around is a great way to strengthen a positive culture in your organization.

Make encouragement, recognition, and gratitude a daily part of your routine. Get intentional and take the 35 Days of Encouragement Challenge. Your organization, your family, your peers, your spouse, your children, and your team will be extremely grateful!!

EXERCISE

Take the 35 Days of Encouragement Challenge. Keep a diary during that time, and note some of the things you see happening due to a more intentional focus on encouragement and gratitude.

INVEST IN DEVELOPING PEOPLE

*Instruct the wise and they will be wiser still; teach the
righteous and they will add to their learning.*
— **Proverbs 9:9 (NIV)**

I still remember how I felt when I was given the opportunity to attend
the Executive MBA program at the University of Minnesota's Carlson
School of Management. It was a huge vote of confidence from my
company and my boss.

It was the early 1990s and I was a vice-president/general manager of
a division of Banta Corporation in Long Prairie, Minnesota. My leader
wanted to prepare me for multi-division responsibility and eventually the
presidency of a group within the corporation.

The simple fact that they were willing to invest in my growth motivated
me to be that much more passionate about continuing to develop my leadership skills. Even more than before, I wanted to be the very best for this
company that was investing in me. I wanted them to have a good payback
for their investment. That is the power of investing in your people!

Servant leaders look for ways to help their team members grow and
develop. That increases the overall competence of the team. But people
also get charged up when they're learning and growing, and that provides
a huge boost of energy.

MAKING MAPLE SYRUP

A few years ago, I started a hobby business producing pure maple syrup. When I started, I knew absolutely nothing about the process. All I knew was that I had a lot of maple trees, and I really liked pure maple syrup.

I started by researching who was producing maple syrup in the Upper Midwest. Then I made a few calls to introduce myself and see if they might share some of their knowledge about the process.

I was blown away by their willingness to share their passion, their knowledge, and their true love for the maple syrup industry. The conversations with these veterans of the industry built my energy so high that now I can't wait for each February to roll around to start tapping trees.

Those industry leaders had lots of things to do. But when I showed up, they dropped everything and shared their knowledge for as much time as I wanted. They gave me tutorials, tours, tips, and insight into industry associations to gain even more knowledge. But most of all, they shared their love for the industry.

It made me think: What if all leaders cared this much about their people? What if we were never too busy to give them the all the time and knowledge that they need? I know we would have more engaged employees. They would know more about their work and work even harder to achieve the organization's goals.

I had a good role model for how a leader like that should act. It was my dad.

LEARNING FROM MY DAD

Some of my fondest memories are of time spent with my dad in the back yard, after he had put in a full day at work. I wanted to be a better baseball player, and he was willing to take the time to help me.

He caught balls while I was pitching, hit grounders to me to work on my fielding, or pitched to me to work on my hitting. Today I know what it is like to put in a full day's work, and I realize how many other things my dad could have been doing. But he took all the time I wanted, giving me tips and providing practice opportunities to develop my skills. That is what servant leaders do!

Some companies are known for the way they develop people. General Electric (GE) has been doing it for more than a century. During that time it's had only eleven CEOs; and every one of them, except of course the founder, Thomas Edison, have come from inside the company.

Companies like GE, Pepsico, and Enterprise Rent-a-Car are known as "academy companies" for the way they invest in developing their people. It should be no surprise that they're also top-performing companies.

Two of my clients are industry leaders in their respective markets, and the way they develop people is a good part of the reason why. Alexandria Industries and Knute Nelson both invest in all kinds of training in technical skills and in leadership.

Several years ago, Lynette Kluver, vice president of organizational development at Alexandria Industries, developed a leadership academy for them. Recently, Knute Nelson created an academy for its own company.

I have had the opportunity to participate in the graduation programs of both academies, and I saw firsthand the incredible level of energy that is being built through development opportunities like them. You will set yourself apart from your competition if you commit to investing in fully developing your people.

There's another benefit, too. Training is the carrier of culture in a company. It's the way you bake in the purpose and values and vision so that they become part of everyone's work, every day. Both Alexandria Industries and Knute Nelson have incorporated servant leadership principles into their leadership academies.

EXERCISE

» Assess how much time, energy, and resources you are expending on developing your people. Then answer the following questions.

» Are you giving them the necessary one-on-one time to share your knowledge, answer their questions, and help them achieve their God-given potential?

» Do you have a process in place to develop leadership and other key skills within your organization to ensure ongoing success?

LEADING JESUS' WAY TO BUILD ENERGY

At that time Jesus came from Nazareth in Galilee
and was baptized by John in the Jordan.
— **Mark 1:9 (NIV)**

Jesus had no followers when He came up out of the Jordan that day. Today, more than two billion people claim His name. In less than a decade, the first believers were spreading the Good News across the world.

You can use the model Jesus created over 2000 years ago for developing leaders. He worked with His senior leadership team in four distinct phases as they developed competence and confidence.

1. I do; you watch.
2. I do; you help.
3. You do; I help.
4. You do; I watch.

Jesus' disciples were not "the best and the brightest." Most of them were subsistence fishermen. There was a tax collector and a revolutionary. In the beginning, all they could do was watch and listen as He taught and preached and healed the sick.

In the beginning, the disciples didn't know what they didn't know. So Jesus' way of working with them was "I do, you watch."

Next, Jesus gave His team small responsibilities: Get the boat across a stormy lake, feed 5,000, rescue a boy from demonic bondage. They often failed and ended up discouraged. They now knew what they didn't know, and Jesus was patient and coached them through with "I do, you help."

As Jesus saw growing competence, He moved to "You do, I help" by granting His 12 (Matthew 10) and then 72 (Luke 10) authority and power to heal and teach. Great things followed, and everyone celebrated. Jesus' students came to know what they knew as they began to put it to practice.

Finally, it was time for "You do, I watch." Jesus delegated His own role to them and passed the torch (Acts 1 & 2).

This model worked with the 12 people He chose for His senior leadership team, who then developed 120 people who went on to **energize** and **develop** the 3,000 converts at Pentecost. From there, the process exploded.

Jesus built energy within His team by constantly clarifying His purpose, values, and vision. He spent time with them, training them to replicate what He was teaching them. He let them know how important they were to the fulfillment of God's overall purpose. He set the boundaries in each of these four phases, and He put them in control of the goal. He encouraged them every step of the way.

His question to you is this: How will you multiply your assets by *energizing* and *developing* the people you are called to lead?

Leading *is* serving; serving *is* leading!

Jesus gave us a powerful model for helping develop team members, but there are some details you should be aware of.

Just like children, people on your team will develop at different rates. Some will develop faster, others slower. Adapt your leadership to each person's unique situation.

Not only that, they each will develop competency in their own unique way and at their own pace, which may be different for each task. When you consider whether it's time to shift from "I do; you help" to "You do, I help," make your decision on a task-by-task basis. Adapt your leadership to each person's unique situation.

EXERCISE

Read Matthew 10, Luke 10, and Acts 1 & 2. Note how Jesus worked with His disciples to build their energy towards accomplishing His purpose. Here are some questions to answer before you move on.

» What are some ways that I could connect the dots for employees to help them understand how important they are to the achievement of our purpose?

» What can I do to allow my people to be creative and be "in control of the goal"?

» How can I raise the level of positive recognition in my workplace and at home?

When you're ready, move on to the section on Building Performance.

BUILD
PERFORMANCE

INTRODUCTION

The Lord does not look at the things people look at.
People look at the outward appearance, but the Lord
looks at the heart.
— 1 Samuel 16:7 (NIV)

Some of my most memorable leadership moments happened coaching my sons' youth baseball teams. That's where I learned that performance is not about being *the* absolute best. Instead it is about being *your* absolute best. If you are striving to be *the* best, you will almost always come up short. Someone, some team, some organization is always better. But you can be *your* best!

I'll never forget the day I allowed a player with special needs to pitch an inning. He did *his* best and turned that day into a very special one in his life. Even today, whenever I see him, he talks about that experience. I see it as the essence of servant leadership.

Your job as a servant leader is to uplift people. When you see more in them than they might see in themselves, it's your job to challenge them and help them. If you do that, they will get to places they would normally not get to on their own. Servant leaders build performance every day!

It isn't easy to build performance every day, to get better every day. I'm constantly amazed that many people think of servant leadership as "soft."

I think they hear the part about building people up and think that's all there is. But it isn't.

Part of your job as a servant leader is to build people up. The other part is to accomplish the mission, whatever it is, through your team. Both jobs are important. Those two jobs are connected. If you build people up, if you help them increase their competence and confidence, it's more likely that you will also get great results. But you may not see those results right away.

That's hard work, filled with hard choices about trade-offs. Another thing makes the work even harder: Servant leaders know that the status quo is not okay.

It doesn't matter how well you're doing right now, you have to keep pressing on to do better. Phrases like "If it ain't broke, don't fix it" or "We've always done it that way" are not tolerated by servant leaders.

We live in a world where everybody is fighting for your customers. There is always more to do and to achieve. If you're not consistently improving, you'll be left behind. So it rests on the shoulders of the leader to foster a culture of continuous improvement.

Examples abound of people or organizations that have rested on their laurels and before they knew it were irrelevant in the marketplace. In 1998, Tom Hall, co-author of *Ruthless Focus*, put together a list of fast-growing companies. He was going to write a book about the lessons you could learn from them.

Other things claimed his attention, though, and he didn't get back to the research and book project until 2008. That's when he discovered something interesting.

Forty-three percent of his "great companies" didn't exist ten years later. Some were acquired by others and some went out of business. Enron was one of them. Yahoo was still around, but never lived up to the promise of those early years. Maintaining success is hard.

The most powerful example of how this works is the US steel industry. Once, US Steel and Bethlehem Steel ruled the roost. But they stuck with old technology and old strategies while other companies, such as Nucor, moved ahead. Today, Bethlehem Steel is gone, and US Steel is a shell of its former self.

Long-term success comes from accomplishing the mission and helping your team members grow and develop while you and your team keep getting better. We've already discussed some of the key parts of that in the sections on Building the Foundation and Building Energy.

Create and share the vision of what the future can be. The team needs to know what they are striving for. This is your job as the leader. You can't delegate it.

Get the work done well every day while driving innovation and improvement. Don't take your eye off the importance of daily execution.

Help your team members do things a little better every day. Remember how Jesus empowered His followers so they could do the work.

1. I do; you watch
2. I do; you help
3. You do; I help
4. You do; I watch

Put people in control of the goal. Often, managers tell people who know the work exactly how to complete a task. You'll get better results and more improvement if you provide teams with the end goal and then allow them to surprise you with ideas and plans on how to get it done. You'll be amazed at what they come up with. The people closest to the action know best what needs to be done to drive improvement. The higher you are in an organization, the fewer decisions you should make anyway.

Make sure everyone knows it's okay to fail. If people sense that there is serious risk to failure, they will not try new things and you will not get significant improvement. Give people a budget and provide incentives for driving improvement and generating new innovative ideas.

Praise people for well-intentioned tries that didn't work out. Utilize every failure for learning opportunity.

Celebrate successes. A culture of continuous improvement requires proper celebration and recognition of those people who are making it happen. I like to encourage leaders to celebrate like they are at a sporting event. Fans don't wait until the end of the game to cheer. They cheer every good play that is made. You should do the same.

Those are important parts of a continuous-improvement culture. In this section you'll learn about some specific things you need to do to increase your team's performance. Here's an overview.

To effectively build performance, get the right people on the team. You're looking for two things. They must be able to do the work and grow with the organization, and their personal values should match up with your organization's values.

Measure the key drivers of your business. It is important to keep score so you'll know if you are improving in those key areas that drive success within your business.

Metrics are very important to people's engagement in their work as well. How long do you think you would bowl, if there was a sheet hanging midway down the alley, which didn't allow you to see how many pins you knocked down, and the electronic scoreboard was shut down? That wouldn't be fun, and I'm guessing you wouldn't keep bowling for long.

The same is true in business. People want to know how they are doing. It is fun, knowing that you are having a good day, and driving improvement for the organization.

Ensure that everyone within your sphere of influence knows what a good day looks like. Make your expectations clear, so that people know what it means to get an *A*. You can't hold people accountable for performance if they don't know what you expect.

You can't build individual and team performance unless you judge what people are doing well and what needs to be improved. Make **performance evaluation** a routine part of your servant leadership.

I've already mentioned the power of the "**Coach Approach**" to leadership. In this section we'll go into coaching techniques in detail so you can coach your people to success.

Servant leaders do a lot of work with individuals, but those individuals do most of their work in teams. This is the section where you'll learn what it takes to lead high performing teams.

EXERCISE

Set the stage for this chapter by completing the following exercise.

» Do a personal assessment on how much you are focusing on your own personal development. What specifically did you do in the last year to enhance your personal performance?

» Now do the same assessment for your work with your team. What specifically did you do in the last year to enhance your team performance?

The results of these activities will give you a baseline reference point as you read the Build Performance section. Turn the page to start the chapter on getting the right people on the team.

GET THE RIGHT PEOPLE ON THE TEAM

One of those days Jesus went out to a mountainside to pray, and spent the night praying to God. When morning came, he called his disciples to him and chose twelve of them, whom he also designated apostles.
— Luke 6:12–13

Jesus spent an *entire night* in prayer before deciding on His senior leadership team. It was important for Him to choose the right people. That's a great example for us.

I've had the opportunity to work with a number of extremely special leadership teams over the years. One of my favorites was our team when I was leading a printing plant in Long Prairie, Minnesota. That group accomplished things that no one dreamed were possible in our industry.

In just about a year and a half, we built a new 315,000-square-foot facility. Then we moved our entire web offset press operation from the old plant to the new one. We never missed a single customer deadline during that entire time. This was due to competency of leadership, passion for people, and values alignment.

You can't win by yourself. Even if you are an athlete in an individual sport like golf or tennis, you still need a highly qualified team to achieve high performance. Building performance starts with the hiring process. That process will be more effective if people want to work for your organization.

CREATE A GREAT PLACE TO WORK

Servant leaders naturally attract great people to their team. People want to be on a winning team with other good people and with a leader who focuses on ensuring growth and development for their team.

Joe Salo is a client and friend. Joe is the site director at LGC Genomics–Douglas Scientific. He regularly shares the following expectation with his senior leadership team: *"I want you to make this the best year of each of your people's life—personally, professionally, and spiritually."* Who wouldn't want to work for a boss like that?

He is a true servant leader. He models the behavior he wants from his team by being absolutely passionate about their development in all aspect of their lives. He has clearly articulated his team's purpose, values, and vision. He challenges them with lofty goals and puts them in control of how to get it done. And they do a lot of celebrating of great performance and milestones met along the way!

He also promotes and provides opportunity for giving back to the community, and he leads a bible study in their workplace for people who are interested. It's obvious to everyone that he truly cares about the well-being of his people. It is no wonder he has a long list of applicants for any job opening within his organization.

When you focus on the greater good for your employees, you will naturally attract the top talent available. Top talent leads to organizational success!

I recently read an article about Southwest Airline's 41-year profitability streak. That's unheard of in the airline industry. What separates Southwest Airlines from the pack? It has to be the people.

People make the difference for Southwest. All the airlines fly the same planes. They go in and out of the same airports. They all have to deal with the same weather and the same fuel prices and the same regulations.

As anyone who has flown Southwest knows, you could be blindfolded and know you were on a Southwest flight. Just about every flyer I know has one or more Southwest stories. I've seen flight attendants in costume on Halloween. I've heard them sing the safety instructions. Southwest has a culture where "fun" is one of the key values.

A culture like this is built intentionally; it does not happen by accident. It starts with the hiring process. At Southwest they want to hire people who want to have fun. So one of the first things they look for is a sense of humor and they have designed the hiring process to make sure they hire people who have one.

Southwest thinks their employees will be the best judge of whether they want to work with a candidate. So groups of Southwest employees interview every candidate. That's how Southwest Airlines winds up with people who fit their values.

HIRE FOR VALUES

The most effective way you build your desired culture is by **hiring for values ahead of competency**. I am not suggesting hiring an English major to do the work of a Chemical Engineer or vice versa. Southwest wouldn't hire an incompetent pilot just because he or she had a sense of humor.

People often ask me how you put this into practice. Start with the foundational work of establishing crystal clear **behaviorally defined values** for your organization. Here's an example.

VALUE: Mutual Respect—*We treat each other with consideration, compassion, and appreciation in all aspects of our relationships.*

ASSOCIATED BEHAVIORS:

> » I will support the consensus of my team by my words and actions.
> » I will practice self-discipline by keeping my emotions under control.
> » I will earn trust through honesty and integrity in all I do.
> » I will accept responsibility and apologize when I have eroded trust.
> » I will be constructive, respectful, and supportive of others.

Once this heavy lifting is done, it's easier to tell if an applicant's values are aligned with the organization's values. Here are three ways to discern values during the interview process:

Use values-aligned behaviorally based questions. For the value of *Mutual Respect* you could ask questions such as these:

» How do you typically react when things don't go as planned within your team?
» Describe a time when you clearly made a bad decision that had an impact on your team, and how you handled it.
» What are people doing when they frustrate you?

Get many points of view. Have as many people as possible talk to potential team members, all with the idea of discerning the applicant's values. Different people detect different things. And if you use team interviewing, everyone else can be observing while one person asks a question.

Get to know the applicant personally. This is all about observation and seeing how they interact. Get potential team members out of the office or work setting. Take them to dinner. Meet their spouse and family. Observe their behavior in personal settings such as sporting events, time with their family, and time with friends.

Values matter more than anything in an organization. Values define the culture, and "**Culture eats strategy for lunch!**" So doing whatever is necessary to ensure that new employees are aligned with the values will be time well spent. It will perpetuate your desired culture and build performance.

I saw a great example of this when my older son, David, entered the workforce after college. One company contacted him for an interview while he was in the middle of his junior year because he was the captain of the university's hockey team.

Federated Insurance had found their best values-alignment results with athletes, and specifically captains of the teams. They put my son through several rigorous interviews, including exposure to different members of their team over a period of a year and a half.

The entire process was designed to determine whether his values were in alignment with the organization's values. They knew they would train him once he was on board. This organization is a leader in its market, and its hiring practice is a big reason. The company commits to a process and is always recruiting, whether or not there are open positions.

This understanding of the importance of values alignment is just as vital when you are a job applicant. As an applicant, always move the interview discussion to clear delineation of how your values align with the values of the organization.

I saw a great example of this when my younger son, Dan, graduated from Iowa State University (ISU) as an industrial engineer at the height of the economic downturn in 2008. All engineers coming out of ISU are extremely qualified and have many great projects and internships under their belts. Most of them focus on those projects and experiences in their interview. My son decided that values were more important.

He moved the conversation to values alignment during every interview. Result: my son interviewed with four companies and received four job offers. Leaders are drawn to people who understand the organization's values and who demonstrate the alignment.

Servant leaders invest the time, effort, and energy to attract great people to their team. They do that by creating a *great* place to work and hiring for values alignment.

EXERCISE

Develop a specific hiring process to ensure that you are hiring for values alignment. What questions will you ask to gain an understanding of values?

SET EXPECTATIONS FOR YOURSELF

All hard work brings a profit, but mere talk leads only to poverty.
— **Proverbs 14:23**

I have been a goal-oriented person my whole life. I was fortunate to work for high-performing organizations where I learned to establish new goals every year to drive both my personal development and organization improvement. One of the greatest learning opportunities for me came when my employer supported my attendance at an Executive MBA Program at the Carlson School of Business at the University of Minnesota.

For six months, I spent a week every month with about twenty-five other executives. We spent twelve to sixteen hours a day in class and studying. At the end of each week, we left with a ton of homework to get done during the three weeks before the next class.

That was hard work, and it meant spending time away from Kim and our young children. Without her commitment to carrying a lot of the parenting load when I was away, or even home and studying, I don't know if I could have done it. But we both knew it was necessary for my continued leadership and business development.

You can't win by yourself. To be successful as a servant leader, you need a team around you. And you're more likely to succeed if they know what you expect.

MODEL THE BEHAVIOR YOU WANT FROM TEAM MEMBERS

Servant leaders work at building performance in every area of their life. If you expect improvement within the team you lead, you have to show the way. You have to model the self-improvement you want, so that the people around you know what it looks like.

Sometimes, when I describe that executive MBA program to another person, he or she gets lost in thinking that they don't have that kind of opportunity. Instead of thinking about how they can grow and develop as a leader, they start thinking about what they can't do. That's a sinkhole. Focus on what you can control, and don't worry about those things you can't control.

I have a hobby maple syrup operation. I understand that I can't control the weather, and therefore the timing of the sap run each year. That is clearly out of my control, so I just don't worry about it. Instead I prepare. I can control the preparations so we are ready when the sap starts flowing.

CREATE A GROWTH ENVIRONMENT

You need to get yourself into a growth environment if you want to get the most from your development efforts. Surround yourself with high performers and with people who want to grow and who will challenge you. That won't always be comfortable; but growth means change, and change is rarely comfortable.

In 2004 I hired Chris Edmonds as a culture coach to help me learn how to change and drive a positive culture within an organization. Chris challenged me and held me accountable. He told me what I needed to hear, instead of what I wanted to hear.

The coaching helped me grow as a servant leader. If I hadn't taken the initiative to create an environment of growth where I was challenged and held accountable for my personal growth, I would not be in a position today to help others in the area of servant leadership and culture improvement. Creating a growth environment will deliver many benefits for you, personally.

Taking control of your personal growth will

» Enhance your skills to enable you be the best you can be for the people you serve,
» Keep your mind active and learning,
» Keep you from becoming lazy and complacent, and
» Enhance your ability to make a significant positive impact in society.

My coaching was also a powerful message for my team. It demonstrated my commitment to personal growth, and it showed how important I thought it was.

Here are some ideas for creating an environment for personal growth:

» Commit to a personal annual goal process.
» Attend leadership training opportunities.
» Hire a coach.
» Ask someone you respect to mentor you.
» Read great books.
» Read great leadership blogs.

GOAL PROGRAM AND ANNUAL FOCUS FOR PERSONAL DEVELOPMENT

Each year I develop an annual goal program for myself to continue to advance my personal performance in the key responsibility areas of my life. I also pick a word or phrase that keeps me focused on my annual development.

My key phrase for 2015 was "All In!" I used that phrase as a reminder to keep doing the things I needed to every day. At the end of every day, I examined my behavior with the following questions:

» **Purpose**—was I "All In" today in working towards the advancement of my purpose?

» **Values**—was I "All In" today in how I behaved and displayed my core values?
» **Physical health**—was I "All In" in my fitness routine and eating habits?
» **Spiritual health**—was I "All In" in spending time in the Word and in prayer to raise the bar on my faith and relationship with Jesus?
» **Mental health**—how did I go "All In" today to enhance the development of my mind and leadership abilities?
» **Relationships**—did I go "All In" today to build relationships with family, friends, clients, and co-workers?

I committed to going "All In" throughout 2015. I wanted to be the very best I could be for my family, friends, and clients. They all deserved the best, so I needed to be "All In" in all I did.

That was my commitment for 2015. But Ken Blanchard likes to say that he doesn't worry about your commitment—he worries about your commitment to your commitment. In other words, will you keep your commitment every day? Well, I can tell you that if you expect perfection, the answer will be "No." We are flawed human beings in all we do; that's why we need Jesus.

There were days where I was indeed "All in." And there were days when I struggled with everything on my list. When I looked back at 2015, though, I could see a few patterns.

I performed best on *physical health*. I've stuck to my exercise routine, and Kim and I have adopted a healthier eating style. The result is that I was in much better shape and had better energy at the end of 2015 than I did at the beginning.

I did pretty well on *spiritual health* and *relationships*, too. *Mental health* was fine from the perspective of reading and learning.

You can't be perfect, but you can get better. And you'll keep discovering new things to work on. For example, I got so caught up in writing this book, developing servant leadership curriculum, and growing my Triune Leadership business that I got out of balance.

I hate to admit it, but I actually took my laptop to the deer stand with me. I put it down to shoot the deer, and I got a lot of work done while I was waiting, but I know this is something I have to work on. Sure, I had answered some emails and caught up on some work, but I also squandered an opportunity to disconnect from work and re-energize.

Here are some things to think about as you set up your goals and annual focus:

» Set a theme or slogan. A simple word or phrase can help you stay focused.
» Review your performance regularly.
» Understand that you will never be perfect.
» Pray for guidance and help.
» Watch for signs of things you should focus on next.
» Review and revise your goals every year.

YOUR LEADERSHIP MOUNT RUSHMORE

I feel every leader needs to establish a *Leadership Mount Rushmore.* Mount Rushmore features the likenesses of four great American presidents, carved into the granite mountainside. Your Leadership Mount Rushmore should be your memories of a few great mentors and role models.

My Leadership Mount Rushmore starts with my dad for his work ethic, faith, and focus. My best boss, Ron Musil, is there for his understanding of what is truly important: building relationships. Next to Ron is my culture coach, Chris Edmonds, for his deep knowledge and guidance on how to build a purpose-driven, values-based culture. My mom, as well as my wife, Kim, round out my Leadership Mount Rushmore for their amazing model of love and always looking for how they can serve others.

The people on your Leadership Mount Rushmore don't have to be part of your everyday life. A friend of mine draws inspiration from a man who was a mentor early in his life, but who died several years ago. My friend says, "There isn't a day that goes by that I don't ask myself, 'What would Leonard tell me to do if he were here right now?' and it always helps."

The people whose behavior we use as a guide are *role models*. If we're lucky, we may be able to have a role model as a mentor. A mentor is a more experienced or more knowledgeable person who guides you in your life or career.

For the last few years, Vern Anderson has been both a friend and a mentor for me. We met working on a community project. Vern has built a successful packaging-equipment manufacturing business, so when I was thinking about leaving the corporate world and starting Triune Leadership Services, I asked him for advice.

I've learned a lot from him about how to succeed in business. But I've learned most from his example of not separating his faith and his work.

Vern has modeled that for me. He's coached me in how to bring Jesus into the workplace and into my daily activities. He's also been a true friend, asking tough questions, challenging me, and cheering me on as I established and built Triune Leadership Services.

Here's what to look for when you're looking for a mentor:

- » Someone who believes in you
- » Someone who will speak the truth to you and to whom you will listen
- » Someone who will give you a picture of the kind of person you want to be
- » Someone who will help you set goals and push you towards them
- » Someone who will hold you accountable for your commitments

To be effective in pursuing great people in your life, I would encourage you to do the following:

- » Pray earnestly for God to put the appropriate people around you.
- » Be intentional and take initiative to pursue them—they won't normally come to you.

- » Start looking within your current relational network.
- » Be willing to ask for advice and help.
- » Realize that some mentors may need to be virtual.
- » Make time in your schedule to make the mentor relationship happen.

Don't take your mentors for granted. Be sure they know how much they are appreciated and the difference they have made and are making in your life.

BECOME A TEACHER

The culmination of personal development is teaching what you have learned. You can sum up the life cycle of development in the following phrase.

"Get it, grow it, give it."

The first step is to *get it*. You can learn great servant leadership skills any number of ways, but it usually doesn't just happen. You can *get it* through great mentors. You can get ideas about what to do from leadership books and training classes. Coaches can help you learn from your experience. I hope this book will help you *get it*.

Remember that servant leadership is a "doing discipline." It's more like riding a bike or swimming than it is like history. You have to do it to learn it. That takes us to the next step.

After you *get it*, the challenge is to *grow it*. Practice the behaviors of servant leadership and make them a part of your daily routine. Practice is a lot of hard work because being a true servant leader normally does not come naturally.

You will make mistakes. That's natural. As legendary teacher Marva Collins would tell her kids, "If you can't make a mistake, you can't make anything." Try things. Get feedback. Reflect on your performance. And try again.

The last area of moving to high performance is to *give it*. Once you are proficient at anything, practice good stewardship and share your knowledge with others to help them grow and make a positive impact on society. Teaching others is a great way to continue to hone your skills. By doing so, you are lifting others up; and that's what servant leadership is all about.

The phrase "Get it, grow it, give it" is a great, easy way to be *intentional* about becoming the most proficient, high-performing leader that your people deserve you to be. No matter where you are in your development, there is always more to get, grow, and give. That is the fun and challenging part.

Servant leaders have a never-ending passion to develop their leadership skills so they can be the very best for the people they serve.

EXERCISE

» Develop three goals for yourself to enhance your leadership skills in the next six months. Commit them to writing and share them with an accountability partner.

» Identify a mentor or coach who will agree to partner with you in your development activities.

SET EXPECTATIONS FOR THE ORGANIZATION

Again, it will be like a man going on a journey, who called his servants and entrusted his wealth to them.
— Matthew 25:14

You've probably heard the saying, "What gets measured gets done." I like that, but I don't think it goes far enough. I like to say, "What gets measured gets improved."

When the master returned from his journey, he asked each servant, "What have you done with what I gave you?" He expected improvement. That's what God expects from us. He expects us to take the gifts He's entrusted to us and make things better. That's your challenge as a servant leader: to help make things better.

GOD EXPECTS US TO MAKE THINGS BETTER

There's only one way I know to make things better in your organization: Create and share clear, reasonable, and measurable expectations and performance goals. Then measure performance and hold people accountable. Here's an example of how that worked for me.

When you're printing magazines and catalogs like my company was, paper waste is a big deal. How well you control that waste can make the difference between making money or not. It's a key variable, so it was one of the important things we measured.

We had standards for every single job we ran, for how fast it should run on the press, how much time it should take to make ready the press, how much paper it should use, and so forth. I could look at my control dashboard and see how much paper we wasted versus how many impressions that we produced by press, by shift, or by operator.

The supervisors could see how they were doing, and so could the individual press operators. They got daily feedback on how they were doing.

That's the basic system. We set goals and tracked performance in key areas. Then we measured how we were doing every day, looking for ways to do better. The result was that we improved performance in our key measures every year.

You may not have the kind of sophisticated measurement technology we had, but you can keep getting better if you set clear goals and expectations, monitor performance, and work to improve.

Servant leaders do not allow people or teams to become complacent. They recognize it is up to them to build an environment of continuous improvement. They start with one key principle.

Status Quo is NOT OK!

Have you ever been on a team where it seemed that nobody wanted to change, where everyone was comfortable proceeding "as is"? They're comfortable in the present and looking to the past for validation. It's a big problem when people are stuck in the past, because their actions block progress and improvement.

LIVING IN THE PAST DELAYS PROGRESS

A servant leader must always be on the lookout for this paralyzing environment. Things may seem like they're going smoothly. The team might even be "meeting expectations." But it's a sign that you're in trouble when you hear things like this:

» "This is how we have always done it."
» "That won't work."
» "I've already tried that."
» "I'm not qualified to make that decision."
» "It seems to be working just fine, the way it is."

When you hear that, it's time to take action. Your attitude makes a big difference in how your team looks at progress and the need for forward momentum. You need to encourage risk-taking, challenge people to figure out improved processes and procedures, provide development opportunities, treat mistakes and failures as learning opportunities, and celebrate successes both big and small.

SERVANT LEADERS STAY FOCUSED ON A BETTER FUTURE

Here are some questions you can ask to help your team focus on making progress and maintaining forward momentum:

» "What can we learn from this experience to make it better next time?"
» "We need to increase output by 5%. What needs to be done to make that happen?"
» "What can I do better to improve this situation?"
» "Do we have best practices that we can apply in other areas?"
» "How will we celebrate when we accomplish this goal?"
» "What are you learning that would help others grow if you shared it?"

Your attitude will be contagious. If you're looking out the windshield instead of the rearview mirror, other team members will start doing the same thing. When people know that risk-taking is rewarded, mistakes are learning opportunities, and wins are celebrated, they will want to join you in the efforts to create a better future.

CREATE A PROCESS TO DRIVE PROGRESS

Attitude is not enough. You need a process that results in positive action. Here are some things I've learned to help you build organization performance.

Set Expectations

You want to stretch people out to levels of discomfort. No growth, learning, or progress takes place without discomfort. So set challenging but reasonable goals.

If you expect little, you will get little; but if you expect a lot, people will stretch and grow to meet the expectation. They will appreciate you for bringing out the best in them. And they will love it when you celebrate a win, especially if it's a big win.

Those big wins are like winning the Stanley Cup in hockey. There's no easy way to win the Stanley Cup. It's a grind. You're the leader, so your job is to embrace the grind and maintain momentum.

Those big wins feel incredible. Don't set expectations too low and inhibit the opportunity for your team to have this amazing feeling. Make challenging expectations part of your annual goal program.

Develop an Annual Goal Program

Start with your purpose and vision and determine the key areas you want to improve in the upcoming year. Then align your entire team around those areas by expecting each leader to develop at least one goal within each key improvement area. Here are some areas where you might set improvement goals:

- » Culture
- » Performance
- » Finance
- » Team-member development

The goals that are established should be SMART. Lots of people use that acronym in goal setting and there are many different versions. In fact, one researcher has documented over 900 of them. When I say goals should be SMART, I mean they should be

- » Specific,
- » Measurable,
- » Actionable,
- » Relevant and realistic, and
- » Time-bound.

I published a Goal Book each year that had everyone's goals in it and had room for quarterly updates. This drove teamwork and accountability to encourage everyone to achieve their goals, so the overall team could celebrate like they won the Stanley Cup.

MEASURE EVERY DAY

What gets measured gets improved. Identify the key performance areas in your organization so you can spend your time and effort improving things that will really make a difference. Then measure them.

Measure performance every day. I had a daily dashboard so that everyone in the organization would know how we were doing and how they were contributing. You don't need sophisticated technology. For many years, salespeople have used Beat Yesterday books to improve their performance. Sam Walton used one his whole life.

Don't try to measure everything, just the vital few things that make a difference. You may have heard of the 80/20 rule, sometimes called Pareto's Law. It states that a small percentage of activities, say 20 percent, drive a whole lot of results, say 80 percent. Joseph Juran called those activities "The Vital Few." That's what you need to identify and measure.

For my catalog and magazine printing company, paper waste was one of the Vital Few. The Vital Few are different for every industry and slightly different for every company within that industry. Individual teams have a Vital Few, too, and so do individual workers. It may take some effort and time to identify the Vital Few, but the analysis will pay off.

Here's how it worked for Southwest Airlines. Their business model was based on low fares, so keeping the cost per passenger down was important. They figured that one key driver of low cost per passenger was high aircraft utilization. The primary driver of that was quick turnaround time. So that's what they measured and analyzed for, every flight, every day.

Here are some examples of key indicators for organizations in different industries.

Many commercial real estate firms track the number of prospecting calls every day. Many pharmaceutical companies track physician visits for each sales rep. A professional services firm might measure billable hours. A human resources manager could identify training hours as a key measure. A community service organization could measure meals served. A wholesaler could measure backorder percentage. Limit the number of things people have to concentrate on every day to three.

Identify key performance measures for your organization or your team. Identify the important performance measure for each person. Track those every day. That may seem like overkill, but the more you focus on what you want, the more likely you will get it. Keep what is important in front of your team—every day.

EXERCISE

Develop a list of the key metrics in your business. Do you have specific goals for each of those key metrics? How will you measure them every day?

PERFORMANCE EVALUATION

As iron sharpens iron, so one person sharpens another.
— **Proverbs 27:17**

Performance evaluation got much easier for me once I learned the importance of clearly defined purpose, values, and behaviors, as well as clear performance expectations. Once you've set and communicated those key parts of the foundation, managing performance gets a lot easier.

When expectations are clear, you don't have to debate them. The conversation shifts to whether or not people are doing what they're expected to do. I can tell you that I no longer lose sleep when I have to let someone go because of poor performance. If I've done my job of making expectations clear and have given them consistent feedback on their performance, then they reap the consequences of their actions.

One great leader put it this way: "I never fire people. They fire themselves by not performing or behaving badly. I just deliver the message and do the paperwork."

Servant leaders understand that feedback is a vital aspect of building performance. People need to know where they stand, what is going well, and where they can improve.

Everyone craves fair, candid, and caring feedback about their performance. The sad truth is that many people have never gotten that kind of feedback. And many leaders have never learned how to give it.

Your feedback is fair when expectations are clear and reasonable. Fairness is also about consequences. People will accept correction and discipline if they feel that the praise or punishment fits their actions and if they feel that everyone is fairly treated.

Your feedback is candid when you tell the truth and describe things accurately. This is honesty, but it's not "brutal honesty." It's compassionate honesty. You should tell the truth, but never be intentionally hurtful.

Your feedback is caring when it's delivered in the spirit of servant leadership. Tailor your feedback to the individual and the situation. Make sure your feedback will help the team and the individual team member to do better next time.

Giving fair, candid, and caring feedback is one of the ways you serve as a leader. Here are some keys to getting it right.

Provide frequent feedback. If you are around your people a lot, you will notice things that need improvement or that cry out for praise. Seize the moment.

Have regular one-on-one meetings with your team members. Set aside time to meet with individual team members every week or two to discuss their performance, behavior, and goals. Treat the one-on-ones as high priority meetings.

Results should always be measured against clear and agreed-upon performance and values expectations. If you don't do this, it's impossible to be fair.

Feedback should be candid, clear, and focused. Give feedback on specific behavior or performance. That means things that can be observed or measured.

Explore and acknowledge their viewpoints. Do this early in the conversation. You may discover you have the facts wrong or that there's a good reason for what happened. Start by telling your team member what you're going to discuss and why it matters. Then wait for them to speak.

Celebrate successes. The purpose of feedback is to improve performance and behavior. Too many bosses think that means correcting team members and nothing more. But legitimate praise is the most powerful tool you have to do more good things. Catch people doing things right. Then praise them for it.

Develop game plans for improvement in areas where necessary. Some things can be changed after one feedback conversation, but many will take time. When that's the case, develop a simple plan and review progress at every one-on-one.

Follow up. The purpose of feedback is to get performance or behavior to change. Your work isn't done until that happens. After the conversation, follow up to make sure that the change you agreed to has happened.

Many organizations have an annual performance appraisal system, and for many leaders that's the only time they talk to their team members about performance. That's just stupid. It's impossible to meet the standards of fair, candid, and caring if you do that. And it's impossible to make your feedback the driver of positive change.

Think of it this way. If you're a parent, you don't talk to your child about their behavior once a year. You probably talk every day. So add "frequent and usable" to your guidelines for delivering feedback. I like to use a tool that the Ken Blanchard Companies introduced to me. It is called the Performance/Values Matrix.

The great thing about this tool is that it helps you evaluate both performance and values. The goal is to get everyone to the upper right quadrant on every task they perform.

So often we look only at performance issues and don't factor in the extremely important aspect of how people are behaving in alignment with the organization's values. Of course, expectations for both performance and values must be clarified, articulated, and well understood if you ex-

Performance / Values Matrix

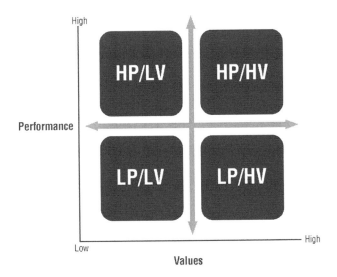

pect the process to be fair. You're never finished with the work of clarifying your expectations. Model them with your behavior. Address them in your one-on-one meetings.

If you're doing that, this matrix is a great tool for determining the direction you will take your discussions. Here are some broad discussion and action guidelines that I suggest by quadrant.

HIGH PERFORMANCE/HIGH VALUES

Consistently let your team members know how much you appreciate the outstanding work they are doing in both areas of performance and values. Offer them more responsibility and more autonomy. Do not ignore these people. One of the most common reasons people leave organizations is that their immediate boss doesn't recognize their good work. Don't give these valuable people a reason to find another place to work.

That's important. You'll be tempted to spend your time on problems and not pay attention to your High Performance/High Values team members. Don't give in. Make the time and effort to tell these people how much you appreciate them.

LOW PERFORMANCE/LOW VALUES

Share these people with your competition just as quickly as possible! You cannot afford to have people on the team who are not delivering on either performance or values.

LOW PERFORMANCE/HIGH VALUES

Do whatever you can to provide training and coaching to help improve their performance. You might have to find a different job for them, one that better suits their skill set. Work diligently to help them improve, because it's hard to find people who are values-aligned with the organization. If after these efforts they still are not performing, you will have to let them go as well. That's a shame, but it's rare. Put in the work and the time to help these people find a productive place in your organization.

HIGH PERFORMANCE/LOW VALUES

This is the toughest group of people. They are doing a great job of delivering on their job requirements, but they are horrible teammates and are not behaving in alignment with the values. You have to keep them on a very short leash, because they can poison the morale of any team.

Explain what it looks like to be on this team, based on the agreed-upon, behaviorally defined values, and make it clear that they are going to fire themselves if they don't change immediately. Work with them and praise their progress; but if they don't change, move quickly to share them with the competition as well. Some of the biggest mistakes I've made involved hanging on to these people too long.

I've had top sales people who were in this quadrant. The sales manager says, "Oh, there's no way we can let that person go, because we'll lose a ton of business." Usually that doesn't happen. You finally make the move and everybody steps up to the plate and picks up the slack. You don't end up losing any accounts, everybody's happier, and people recognize how serious you are about the culture that you want.

It's tempting to hang onto these people because they deliver on the numbers, but the numbers only help for this week or this month or this quarter. And they're destroying morale that's important for the long-term success of the organization. Let them go as soon as you know they're unwilling to change.

Lots of people think of feedback as an event, but it's really part of a full system of performance evaluation. Here's a reminder of what that looks like.

Everything begins with the foundation of purpose and values and vision. You must establish clear performance and values expectations and communicate them over and over. People need to know what you expect from them before you can hold them accountable.

A solid system and cadence of performance discussions will build performance. Servant leaders make this a part of their regular routine and discussions with people. Deliver fair, candid, and caring feedback, then agree on what will change, and follow up to make sure agreement turns into action.

Use the Performance/Values Matrix as a framework for determining the direction of your performance discussions. Remember that you can almost always teach people skills and find a place for them in your organization. That's worth doing if their values align with your values. It's harder to change values. If their values don't align with your organizational values, you will probably have to lovingly set them free.

EXERCISE

Plot your direct reports on the Performance/Values Matrix for each of the tasks they're responsible for.

» Develop a game plan for specific discussions with your people about their performance and behavior.

COACHING

A wise man has great power, and a man of knowledge increases strength; for waging war you need guidance, and for victory many advisors.
— **Proverbs 24:5–6**

I experienced the impact of an executive coach when I first learned the process of driving a purpose-driven, values-based culture from the Ken Blanchard Companies. Throughout that two-year process of learning, Chris Edmonds was my coach. Chris helped me achieve things I never would have without his help. That's what good coaching can do.

I was already an experienced leader at that time in my career. Chris didn't tell me what to do. Instead, he asked the right questions to get me to discover new, more effective ways of leading, ways that would institutionalize our desired culture. He also held me accountable for my commitments. He was the accountability partner I had to report to every month.

When I left the corporate world to start Triune Leadership Services, I knew I wanted to be an effective executive coach to help other leaders. I had experienced what coaching can do, and I was convinced that taking a coach approach to leadership was fully in line with servant leadership. After all, true coaches are 100 percent focused on the greater good of the people they coach. Sounds like servant leadership to me!

WHAT I LEARNED FROM FORMAL TRAINING IN COACHING

I knew what I wanted to do, but I still had a lot of questions. I knew there were several certification programs for coaches, but I didn't know if they were necessary or, if they were, which course was the right choice for me. After I did a little research on my own, I reached out to Linda Miller for advice.

Linda is a Master Certified Coach who serves as the Global Coaching Liaison for the Ken Blanchard Companies. She convinced me that it was important to be perceived as a quality coach and that a certification program would give me a credential and also help me develop my coaching skills.

The program I chose took a year and a half to complete, and I was certified in 2012. What I learned made a huge difference in my business and my life. I really wish I'd had that training thirty years ago, because I would have been a better boss and a better parent. I would have been a better servant leader, too. I learned a lot, but three lessons stand out from the rest.

> » **I learned how important it is to listen well. Listening is a skill you can really work on.** If you work hard, you will get better. The better you get at listening, the more influence you're going to have, and the more effective you're going to be at coaching people.
> » **Asking great questions complements listening.** So, what's a great question?
> » **A great question leads a person into discovery.** It kind of knocks them off-center and helps them understand things differently from before.

Great coaching is not about trying to figure things out for the individual. It's all about coming in with no answers, then asking the good questions and really listening to the answers. I've had formal training in the techniques, because coaching is part of my business and I want to be the best coach I can be. But anyone can learn and use the basics of coaching to become a more effective servant leader.

I've developed training to help leaders take a Coach Approach to their leadership. The feedback I have received from leaders is overwhelming as to the positive impact it has made in their leadership effectiveness. I know it's a big promise, but that feedback and my own experience have led me to believe that if you develop good coaching skills you will be more successful and happier in just about every aspect of your life.

MAKE TIME FOR ONE-ON-ONE MEETINGS

As you develop those critical questioning and listening skills, you can make some changes in the way you structure your work as a leader. Start by taking the time for one-on-one meetings with your people.

The number one reason people leave organizations is that they feel neglected and unappreciated by their immediate supervisor. Making the time to conduct regular one-on-one meetings with your people will ensure true connection. It is really the *only* way to effectively coach them to build performance. Here are some of the advantages and outcomes of one-on-one meetings:

- » People feel respected and that their work is worthwhile.
- » People stay focused on the purpose, values, and vision of the organization.
- » A clear understanding of expectations and priorities is maintained.
- » People are allowed time to weigh in on how I could improve my effectiveness as a leader.
- » Time is dedicated to the individual and his or her development.
- » It is a great model for others to follow.

I think it's a good idea to use a standard structure for your one-on-one meetings. I usually start with a check-in and a review of commitments on both sides. The agenda should be dictated by the person you are meeting with. Here are some guidelines for what to do.

Listen more than you talk—a lot more. This illustrates and builds trust. Ask great questions such as these:

> » What is the greatest challenge you currently face?
> » What have you found to be effective in working on this goal?
> » How would you describe your team's engagement and morale?

Celebrate wins. Provide specific recognition for the work that has been done. Be sure to say thank you.

Coach, direct, or train based on the person's level of knowledge, engagement, and passion on an issue. Tailor your approach to their needs and wants.

Before you wrap up the meeting, establish commitments and a game plan that will be acted upon before the next one-on-one. That's how you ensure consistent progress.

I usually met one-on-one with my direct reports every two weeks. That frequency worked well for me. There was enough time between one-on-one sessions to make significant progress. But the time was short enough to catch problems while they were still small.

I kept the meetings with each individual on the same day and time, so it was not only part of my cadence but theirs as well. If we weren't located in the same office, the meetings might be phone conversations, but I tried to travel to see people as often as possible.

You *must* keep your commitment to having these meetings. Your credibility as a leader depends on it! Put them on your calendar as recurring events. Then don't change them unless there's a very good reason. Remember: This is part of the real work of servant leadership.

Regular one-on-ones can be an important part of your personal life, too. I encourage you to set aside scheduled connection time for your spouse, children, and friends, anyone who's important in your life.

HELP PEOPLE TAKE CONTROL

Taking a Coach Approach to your leadership reinforces the idea that you don't do all the work. Instead, you're helping team members develop so they can do their work with minimal supervision. If you feel your load getting heavy and everyone seems to come to you for problems to be solved and decisions to be made, you probably need to focus on being a better coach instead of being that person with all the answers.

When people see you as the only person who can make a decision, you become a bottleneck for the organization's progress and the development of future leaders. Realistically, the farther up the organization chart you go, the less you know about the day-to-day realities of the work below you. Servant leaders recognize this and focus on building their team members' competencies. They tell others, "You decide."

Putting people in control of their own destiny is much more sustainable than having you, as a top leader, making all the decisions. Plus it allows you to focus on what you do best, which maximizes your impact. Listen intensively, acknowledge other ideas, ask powerful questions that will promote further discovery, and encourage every team member to reach for the best!

Don't allow people to push decisions up. When they come to you for an answer or specific direction, consider these possible responses:

- » What are you thinking about your possibilities?
- » What do your instincts tell you?
- » Maybe there isn't just one answer.
- » My answer might not be right for you.
- » This is about you, not about me.
- » I have confidence in you. Your solution is best. Let's go for the best!

The more effective you are in serving your team as a coach, the more you are able to focus in your own personal areas of strength, and the greater your influence and significant impact will become.

EXERCISE

Develop a schedule to meet regularly with your direct reports. Take a Coach Approach to those meetings by effectively listening and asking powerful questions to help your people build performance and achieve their dreams.

BUILD A HIGH PERFORMING TEAM

Two are better than one,
because they have a good return for their labor:
If either of them falls down,
one can help the other up.
But pity anyone who falls
and has no one to help them up.
                    — Ecclesiastes 4:9–10

If you have ever been on a high performing team, you know the magic that can exist. I have had the opportunity to be a part of numerous great teams. Earlier I mentioned the team we had in the printing plant in Long Prairie, Minnesota. Another great example is the team from one of my first roles as a customer service manager in a printing plant in Pontiac, Illinois.

I was about a year and a half into my career when I got promoted from service rep to customer service manager. About a dozen customer service representatives reported to me, and most of them were veterans of the business who had been in that role for many, many years. Later on, I brought in some people right out of college to bring fresh energy to the team.

I was fortunate, because my dad was in the printing business and I'd been around it my whole life, so I knew how competent those team members were. Even though I was technically the leader, those people knew way more than me about how to do the work. So it seemed natural to build on the strengths of those elder statesmen. I think I was practicing servant leadership then, even though I'd never heard the term.

Servant leaders understand it's never about any one individual; it's about the team. You cannot accomplish great things on your own; it takes an entire team of people pulling together towards a common purpose with common values. When you get everyone pulling in the same direction, you can accomplish great things.

You can have all the talent in the world, but it might not equate to success. Teamwork is the key!

Tom and Kristi Schabel are good friends whose daughter Taylor's 4 X 100 relay team won the Minnesota High School State Championship in 2014. When they asked for prayers for their team in advance of the State Final, they did not ask people to pray for them to run the fastest; they asked for prayers on the baton exchanges.

Passing the baton may look easy, especially when it's done smoothly, but doing it well requires a lot of practice. Two runners need to match their speeds so they are together near the end of a specific "changeover zone." That means one runner has to start running when the incoming runner passes a specific check point. They have to pass the baton smoothly, so the outgoing runner never breaks stride. It takes hours of practice to get this right for every pair of runners. That's the teamwork part of the relay race.

Without a focus on teamwork and smooth handoffs from one team member to another, these four girls could have been the fastest individually in the state and not won the race. Instead they are state champions because they concentrated on being a great *team*!

Servant leaders understand the importance of teamwork. They recognize that "All of us are always smarter than any one of us." Servant leaders capitalize on each individual's strengths and then maximize the efficiency of the coordination and transitions between them.

I've identified these *six key components for developing high-performing teams*:

Leadership and followership. High-performing teams have a great leader and team members who are engaged and passionate about the leader's vision for the team.

Purpose, values, and vision. Everyone on the team understands the purpose of the team, what they want to create in the future, and how they are going to behave with each other on their journey.

Norms that clarify acceptable behavior. Everyone honors and respects each other with positive encouraging behavior. Norms define how we're going to work together as a team. They include things like what we're going to do with our cell phones during meetings. One client team I work with has written out its norms and prints them on the back of every meeting agenda.

Clear understanding of team and individual responsibility. Everyone takes the necessary responsibility and is accountable for the team's success.

Goals that stretch the team to new levels of achievement. No one is satisfied with the *status quo*. Instead, everyone always strives to do better and help the team do better.

Communication strategy. High-performing teams develop specific ways they will communicate with each other. Processes are a form of communication, too. They make sure that everyone knows how to do things the same way.

In my experience, these key attributes of a high-performing team do not just fall into place over time. Great teams don't happen by accident. Instead, it takes intentional work together to define and clarify all of the key aspects listed above. Great teams learn to work together. This work will be an ongoing effort, but it will provide a significant return on performance.

Beyond those six components, there are three things you have to pay attention to as the team leader: *meetings, collaboration*, and *team chemistry*.

MEETINGS

Team meetings are the primary way that the team coordinates effort to reach a common goal. I've found four keys to performance-building team meetings.

The first key to effective meetings is to have an agenda and purpose for every meeting that requires the entire team's participation. It's up to you to ensure that meeting time is used for discussion and not reporting. Reporting can be done one on one, or via reports before the meeting. Meeting time should be used to capitalize on the collective brainpower in the room to build ideas, game plans, and solutions.

Agenda items should always advance one of the following:

» Purpose of the organization or team
» Vision of the organization or team
» The team's key responsibility areas (KRAs)
» Culture of the organization

If an agenda item doesn't pass this test, you shouldn't be talking about it at a team meeting.

The second key to an effective meeting is full participation by the team. This requires you to ask relevant questions and actively listen. Think of it as coaching the whole team. You should ask great questions to drive important discussion and discovery within meetings. Here are some examples of good questions.

» What is your read on employee morale, and what are the primary factors leading to that conclusion?
» Where have you seen evidence of people exhibiting company values?
» What have we done in the last week to advance our vision?
» What is happening when you see the organization falling short on our financial expectations? What are things we could do to overcome that situation?
» Where are we seeing the best evidence of leaders being developed? What should we do to enhance our bench strength of future leaders?

Your job as the leader is to build on people's strengths, capitalize on the collective knowledge of the team, promote discovery, raise the bar on performance, and lead. Running effective meetings and talking about relevant topics that will advance the organization's purpose, vision, and culture is an important part of your role as leader.

The third key to effective meetings is to press for closure when decisions need to be made and ensure clarity on accountability moving forward. You should make sure that all decisions and responsibilities are summarized at the meeting and then documented and distributed for accountability purposes.

The last key to effective meetings is to review performance of the meeting with team members at the close of each meeting. Work to improve your performance on meetings, just like you work to get better at anything else.

COLLABORATION

I do a lot of work with senior leadership teams, to help them develop and define their company's purpose and values. This process always reinforces the value of collaboration and the belief that "All of us are always smarter than any one of us."

Teams I have worked with say that they are amazed at the quality of their work and the profound positive impact on the organization when they work together. Effective, intentional collaboration leads to inclusion and clarity in the workplace and demonstrates the importance of people's ideas to drive high performance.

There's another advantage to collaboration: Men and women who work on a truly collaborative team for the first time are usually amazed at how much more satisfying work can be. That's because they get to do more of the things they do well and enjoy. It's a win all around.

Now, I've used the word "collaboration" a lot so far. I want to be clear about what I think collaboration is and is not for a servant leader.

For a servant leader, collaboration is:

» Listening to everyone's perspective whenever possible,
» Sincerely being open to trying new ways of doing things,
» Understanding and acknowledging the strengths of everyone,
» Drawing out the best ideas, and
» Understanding the importance of collaboration and holding that as a key value.

It's also important to know the other side of the coin. For a servant leader, collaboration is not:

» Using hierarchical power,
» Ruling by intimidation or position power, or
» Expecting your ideas to always be selected.

CHEMISTRY

The team with the most talent doesn't always win. Every year in every team sport there are teams who should triumph because they have the best talent but who fall short. Team chemistry is often cited as the reason. Team chemistry is the "X Factor."

Our local high school hockey team takes team chemistry very seriously. Each Wednesday evening during the season they meet at a player's house without coaches to get to know each other better. They also invite a speaker to talk about leadership and personal development. They are intentional about building chemistry within the team.

Some people think chemistry is something magical that you don't have any control over. But our high school hockey team doesn't believe that. They develop team chemistry by the way they spend time together.

In a recent study of top-performing commercial real estate teams, every top-performing team did something *intentional* to develop team chemistry. Some teams had formal team-building events, and all of them had other things that they did together. Here are some examples you can consider.

» Take your team to offsite meetings and events to get them away from the normal day-to-day activities.
» Have some competitive events to build camaraderie within the team.
» Build shared responsibilities into the events so everyone has a leadership role at some time during the event.
» Build a time of relaxation into the event so people can unwind together.
» Allow for a faith component to take the team relationships to another level.

Those are team events, but many teams develop chemistry by just getting together outside of work. That's how it was with my customer service team in Pontiac, Ilinois. We got together virtually every Friday night away from work, with both team members and spouses. We spent a lot of other social time together, too. During that time we developed a chemistry that made us a better team on the job.

High-performing teams understand the importance of being intentional about building chemistry. They know it can be a difference-maker in the level of success they achieve. While a lot of options exist for developing team chemistry, a servant leader needs to focus on a few key activities.

» **See how much you can learn about the members of your team: their past, their present, and their dreams for the future.** Be on the lookout for things you have in common with different team members and that different members have in common with each other.
» **Celebrate accomplishments along the way.** Don't wait for a super-big accomplishment. Celebrate small wins and progress. Look for a unique and powerful way to celebrate. One team in that commercial-real-estate study had "success bells" in the center of their office. When a team member had something to

celebrate, big or small, business or personal, he or she could ring the bells and share their accomplishment with everyone.

» **Express gratitude and appreciation freely.** A thank-you goes a long way. Say it to individuals and the entire team. Handwritten thank-you notes do wonders, too.

» **Constantly look for ways to serve others on the team.** Think of others first, and show your fellow teammates that you value them by assisting them whenever you can.

» **Never stop looking for ways to do life together.** That's the essence of community. It's not about me; it's about we.

» **Be patient.** You may not see results right away. But, if you stay the course and continue to make "deposits," chemistry will grow deeper and deeper over time. The effect is cumulative.

» **Build team chemistry.** It will enhance performance in any area of life. Whether it is in your family, in athletics, in the business world, or in another organization, a team with a high level of chemistry will normally outperform teams who don't have it. The good news is that with some intention you can build a high level of chemistry within your team.

Developing a high-performing team is critical in building performance. Your ability to develop high-performing teams is critical to your success. Today everything happens with a team.

EXERCISE

» Do an analysis of your effectiveness of team meetings with your team. Check to ensure each of the four key components of effective meetings are standard protocol with your team meetings.

LEADING JESUS' WAY
TO BUILD PERFORMANCE

I tell you the truth, anyone who believes in me will do the same works I have done, and even greater works, because I am going to be with the Father.
— John 14:12

Using Jesus as the model for building performance sets the bar extremely high for us. Jesus sets an example that we cannot reach without His help. Remember how it was for the disciples, as told in Matthew 14.

Jesus and His disciples were in a remote place with over 5,000 hungry people. The disciples asked Jesus to send the crowds away so they could go back to the villages and buy their own food. Instead Jesus told His disciples, "That isn't necessary; you feed them."

The disciples thought that was impossible. They answered, "We can't feed them; we only have five loaves of bread and two fish." The disciples probably figured that they were pointing out the obvious. I'll bet Jesus was frustrated with them right then.

Jesus told the disciples to bring Him the bread and fish. He took them, looked up to heaven, and blessed them. Then He broke the bread into pieces and gave it to the disciples to distribute to the people. They fed everyone and wound up with twelve baskets of leftovers.

Do you think Jesus was serious when He asked His disciples to feed the people? I think He was. I also think He was teaching them a lesson. It's a good lesson for us, too. We cannot expect to build performance to the levels Jesus wants without His help!

As leaders, we have all been tossed in over our heads. Whether it is marriage, raising children, or becoming a servant leader, again and again we find ourselves out of our league and expected to do more than we ever have.

That's been true for me over and over. Getting promoted to lead the customer service team in Pontiac is a good example. Some of those reps were old enough to be my father, and all of them knew more than me. To succeed, I had to use Jesus as the model.

Jesus leaned on His Father (God) throughout His life to carry Him through as He delivered on His purpose. That is the example He lays out for us. He has invited us with open arms to communicate daily with Him through the study of scripture and prayer to enable us to build performance in our lives and in His kingdom.

God demands performance beyond our reach, so we must depend on His strength. We know and understand that we cannot do enough on our own. Thinking first and foremost about the greater good of others is unnatural for us. It can only happen by our leading through Jesus in our lives. He can make it happen.

Mark Herringshaw, a good friend and fellow leadership development consultant, shared this simple prayer with me that I think does a great job of summarizing the only way we can expect to build our performance as a servant leader:

I can't.
You can.
Please do.
Thank YOU!

Remember that as you learn to be a faith-based servant leader. Servant leadership doesn't come naturally to most of us. You will be in over your head constantly. You will feel uncomfortable, and you will wonder if you can do the work. You can, with God's help.

Servant leadership is not "soft," and it is not easy. Building performance is absolutely necessary to stay relevant in our world today. Without a leader's demanding it, performance won't necessarily improve. And, if performance doesn't improve, we put ourselves and our teams at risk.

Even so, I believe that building performance is one of the most enjoyable aspects of being a servant leader. Helping people get to places they wouldn't normally get on their own is fun and rewarding. And there is nothing more fun and exhilarating than winning as a team.

That won't happen by accident, though. You must get the right people on your team. Then you have to set clear expectations and work with people in a Coach Approach to help them achieve their goals and team goals. Developing a great team will be hard at first, but you'll build momentum. Soon, you and your team will achieve new levels of performance.

That can happen if you have included the most important team member of all—Jesus. Bring Him onto your team, both personally and professionally. He wants to be there. He has promised to help every step of the way. I invite you to take Him up on that promise. Your ride to new levels of performance will be above and beyond your expectations. *I guarantee it!*

EXERCISE

Pray for Jesus to walk alongside you as you develop your personal skills as a servant leader. Admit that you cannot do it on your own, and that you would cherish His help on the journey. Speak to Him on a daily basis about how it is going. Give thanks for the changes you start to see in your leadership, and for the positive impact you are having on others, through His strength.

BUILD
RELATIONSHIPS

INTRODUCTION

Follow God's example as dearly loved children and
walk in the way of love, just as Christ loved us.
~ Ephesians 5:1–2

I always cared for people I led, as if they were family. After all, I spent more time with them than I did with my own real family. So why not get to know them, love them, and care for them? People want to work for people who care for them. And Jesus tells us to love others just as He loved us.

More than half the Christmas cards we send out each year are to people I have worked with over the past thirty-five years. Building relationships is a big reason for whatever success I had as a leader over those years. That's true of almost all the successful people I know.

Nothing is more important in a servant leader's life than building relationships. We are in a people business, in every aspect of our lives.

In my career, I have observed several highly intelligent leaders who never reached their potential, due to their inability to build relationships. Leaders who don't focus on building relationships send the message that they are too busy or that they don't care. Some of them even treat the people they work with like resources instead of God's children.

The funny thing is, those people usually think what they're doing is concentrating on the work to be done. They don't understand that relationships are the key to getting the work done well and to living a healthy life, too. I often think of one man I knew who was like that.

He enjoyed "holding it over" people that he was the boss. He seemed to enjoy giving orders and catching people doing things wrong. He was also a classic workaholic. Those things are a horrid combination.

This fellow also liked to pretend that he worked harder than anyone else. He got to the office early, and his day was off to a bad start if anyone got there ahead of him. At the end of the day, he stayed in his office until his car was the only one in the parking lot.

I used to challenge that fellow about having some balance in his life. He always said that he could spend time with his family and build relationships when he retired. He never got the opportunity. A heart attack killed him before he would have retired. Whenever I'm tempted to work a little too much, I think about him.

Fortunately, I've worked with many leaders who were good role models for me. They put others first. They valued everyone they worked with, cared about them, and engaged with them. They knew they didn't have to be the one with all the answers and that good ideas could come from anyone.

In this section we are going to examine the ways you can get intentional about building relationships. The most important keys I have found to build relationships effectively are here, each with its own chapter.

- » Create mutual respect and trust
- » Listen
- » Play to people's strengths
- » Coach and train
- » Maintain a positive attitude
- » Be yourself
- » Let Jesus be your model

EXERCISE

Take a moment to list all the people you work with regularly. Then make notes about your relationship with each one. As you read the chapters in this section, make notes about how you can improve each relationship.

MUTUAL RESPECT AND TRUST

As they talked and discussed these things with each other, Jesus himself came up and walked along with them.
~ Luke 24:15

I believe that Jesus walks along with servant leaders. He helps us find the loving way to lead. Sometimes we find guidance in the scriptures and in prayer. Sometimes we find the loving way by following the example of leaders who came before us. My father was one of those leaders for me.

He started working in a newspaper on a linotype machine when he was in high school. Then he went into the Army and served in the Korean War. When he came back, he went back to the printing business and worked his way up to department management. He was a soft-spoken man who led by example.

One example he set was hard work and focus on the customers. We wouldn't see him at the dinner table until the job was done at work. And I was lucky to have the opportunity to watch him at work, because I started working in the plant during high school.

I never saw him chew out anybody, but he had high standards and he expected the people who worked for him to do the job and do it right. This was back when prepress was a craft. He was extremely meticulous in how he did everything, and that's what he expected of everybody.

One of my personal core values is mutual respect and trust, and that comes straight from my dad. He brought me up to have a great deal of respect for others. He said that you build trust through mutual respect. One way you learn to respect others is by "walking in their shoes."

WALK IN THEIR SHOES

I started working in the printing industry when I was fifteen years old. I started at the bottom, and I don't think there's a job I haven't done in the printing business at one time or another. That was fortunate. The experience really helped me build relationships with everyone as I led printing companies.

The printing business has changed a lot in twenty years, just like every other business. Just because I did a similar job twenty years ago doesn't mean I really understand it today. To stay current, I started a simple practice very early in my career.

I periodically picked a different area of the plant to work a few hours or a full shift. This allowed me to gain a present-day understanding of the environment our people were working in and the challenges they faced. I walked in their shoes.

SIX ADVANTAGES OF "WALKING IN THEIR SHOES":

- » People see you struggle with work they do very efficiently.
- » You become a real person to the workforce.
- » You get an opportunity to see things that otherwise might have gone unnoticed.
- » You become another ear for employees to share ideas and concerns.
- » You learn to appreciate the work your people do every day.
- » You build relationships.

I am not saying that in order to be a leader, you have to have held every position that you are now responsible for. I am saying, if you want to maximize your effectiveness and influence, it helps to figure out a way to thoroughly understand the challenges and battles everyone within your organization is facing. You must know that, to serve them as their leader.

SHOW RESPECT

My favorite bosses are those who are not afraid to get down in the trenches and work side by side with the troops. They do so because they greatly respect each and every person and the value they bring to the table. But respecting people isn't enough. You have to demonstrate that respect, and that starts with acknowledging people.

Never walk by someone without acknowledging them. People are always watching you. They're looking for clues about what's important to you and how they should act. If you walk by someone without acknowledging them with at least eye-to-eye contact and a head nod, you have just told that person that you don't care about them. Not only that, you've told everyone who saw you that you don't care about that person. That may be the last thing on your mind, but it is exactly what they are thinking.

I try to be very intentional about this, and there are certainly different levels of acknowledgement. Eye contact and a nod of the head is the bare minimum. Next best would be to say "Hi" and address them by name. Even better, stop for a conversation, ask questions, and listen. You may not have time for conversation, but you always have time for something.

You may only have a minute or two with the people God puts in your path. Use that time to advance your purpose or, even more importantly, to advance God's purpose of eternal salvation for all.

Building relationships is critical for a servant leader. Here are a few things you can do to make it more likely that you will build solid relationships.

> » **Believe that others are more interesting than you.** Demonstrate that belief by showing interest in people and in their work and their life.
> » **Focus on being more interested than interesting.** Think of good questions you can ask.

» **Relationships grow from conversations; so do the things necessary to have more conversations.** I've discovered that you have something in common with every person who works for you. Discover it. Talk about it.

» **Just ask *one* question!** Relationships start with a conversation, and a conversation starts with just one question.

» **Listen**. That's how you show respect, and that's how you learn. You can't learn when you're talking. I'll have more to say about this in the next chapter.

I tried to put those key behaviors together in what I found to be the single most important practice that led to my leadership success. That practice was walking the floor every day. Here are the keys for making it work.

» **Make it a daily routine**. I set aside one hour every morning and one hour every afternoon to get out and talk to people in all areas of the organization. You're more likely to do it if you set aside time and do it every day.

» **Learn everyone's name**. This won't happen in the first week on the job, particularly if you have hundreds or thousands of employees, but with consistent effort it will happen. I have seen leaders use flash cards with every person's picture on the front and names on the back and then have their spouse quiz them every night until they knew every one of their employees by name.

» **Don't get comfortable by always talking with the same people.** This is an easy trap to fall into. Some people will be easy to connect with, others more challenging. You need to make it a point to connect with everyone.

» **Ask discovery questions**. The more you know about individuals, the better job you can do in asking appropriate questions that truly indicate your interest in them. Be alert for clues when you talk with them. Scan the area around the person you're talking to, for pictures and other personal mementos.

» **Thank them for their insights.** Everyone likes to be appreciated. Use this time to build their self-esteem and encourage them.

Here are some more advantages and outcomes that I found when walking the floor:

» People recognize you as a real person who truly cares about their well-being.
» Your being there creates an opportunity for positive recognition and encouragement.
» People are energized by these discussions and respond with their best.
» You will build an atmosphere of "no fear" as people see it is safe and expected to let you know what is on their mind, and their ideas are acted upon.
» You set an example for other leaders and build a culture of mutual respect and trust throughout the organization.
» You are far more informed of what is truly going on in the organization.
» Having regular conversations with people builds trust, so that later it's easier to have difficult conversations about performance or behavior.
» It is good physical exercise.

Your servant leadership skills will grow as you become intentional about building relationships. When you have mutual respect and trust as a core value, you will figure out ways to make connections with people that will build relationships. People are hungry for connection. The results will be beyond your imagination.

EXERCISE

» Commit to learning people's names. Start with people within your span of leadership, and then move to their spouse's names and their children's names.

» Build a routine of taking a tour of your area of responsibility on a daily basis for no other reason than to connect with people.

LISTENING

My dear brothers and sisters, take note of this:
Everyone should be quick to listen, slow to speak
and slow to become angry.
~ James 1:19

Read that verse again. James suggests that we should be "quick to listen" and "slow to speak." I think we get it backwards a lot. Most people think that the leader is the person who should be doing most of the talking. That's not true for servant leadership.

One of my mentors is Vern Anderson, founder and chairman of the board of Douglas Machine, and he's a great listener. He's always willing to listen to anyone who wants to talk to him and ask for his insights. I got to experience that firsthand.

He and I met often when I was thinking about moving out of the corporate world and starting my own business. He listened to my concerns, thoughts, and dreams for what might be possible. He allowed me to articulate my thoughts aloud, which really helped, and he then asked me to be patient and allow God to work through the details to make all my dreams possible. His calm demeanor, as well as his ability to demonstrate that he truly cared about what I was working through, made him someone I truly valued and wanted to talk to.

Servant leaders build relationships. We build relationships that embody mutual respect and trust, and we do that mostly through conversations. Listening is a vital part of effective servant leadership.

Listening helps us learn about the people we work with. You want to know what matters to your people and what challenges they face, so that you can serve them. You can't learn those things while you're talking. Listening is the only way.

The irony is that the better you are as a listener, the more influence you will have as a leader. Your people will know you care about them. They will know you understand what they're facing every day. And so they'll listen to you.

Many of us take listening for granted. I used to be in that camp. I knew listening was important, and I thought I did it pretty well. And I did, in some ways.

I was good at the kind of listening that makes for a good conversation. I didn't understand the difference between that kind of listening and the kind of listening that promotes the growth of the other person. When I went to Coach University, I learned about a different way to listen.

I wish I'd learned to be a better listener decades ago. I would have been a much better leader. But you don't have to wait. Listening is a skill you can start improving today. Being an effective listener is one of the most important attributes of a servant leader. When you listen better, good things happen because you're having good conversations.

» You discover new ideas.
» You recognize the power and value of others.
» Good conversations build energy.
» Good conversations build relationships.

The kind of listening we're talking about is called *active listening*. Here are some things you can do to master this critical skill.

COMMIT TO BEING A BETTER LISTENER

It's easy to "commit" to being a better listener without making much progress. So commit to a *specific way* of listening.

If you want to improve your listening, start by listening 80 percent of the time and talking only 20 percent of the time. Spend half your talking time asking good questions. Use the other half of your talking time to share your thoughts and reactions. If you're doing the math, that's 80 percent listening, 10 percent asking questions, and 10 percent sharing your thoughts and reactions.

Let me sum up the advice: Listen as if you were listening to Jesus. You would spend most of your time listening. You would ask questions to make sure you understood what Jesus was saying. And you would spend some time sharing your thoughts and reactions.

PAY ATTENTION

Our world is filled with distractions. Turn away from your computer screen. Put your phone away. Move to a quiet place or close the door. That's what you would do if you were listening to Jesus. You wouldn't want to miss a word.

ACT LIKE YOU'RE LISTENING

Use silent actions to demonstrate that you're listening. Look at the other person. Lean in to the conversation. Nod to show understanding. Encourage the other person to continue with such simple words and phrases as "Yes" and "Okay." Use sounds, such as "Uh-huh."

Use all senses to indicate a true interest in the individual you are listening to. Appropriate body language, eye contact, and personal space are critical to connecting in a conversation.

RESPOND TO WHAT YOU HEAR

There are several things you can do to respond to what you hear and keep the focus on the other person. Restate or summarize what you've heard in different words, and ask if you've got it right. "Here's what I think you're saying...."

After you've summarized what you're hearing, you can share your reaction. Be respectful and courteous, like you would with Jesus.

USE QUESTIONS EFFECTIVELY

Questions are powerful, so you want to be sure you use them for good. "Why?" questions tend to make people defensive, so try to avoid them. If the person is describing something from the past, ask them what happened. If they're suggesting an action, ask what they think will happen. Either way, you usually get the same kind of explanation that a "Why?" question would generate, but without the emotional response.

Use open- and closed-ended questions effectively. Open-ended questions have many possible answers. "How did that work out?" "How did you feel when that happened?"

Closed-ended questions have a limited number of responses. "Were you talking with Tom or was it Mary?" "How many people were in the room?" "What day was that?" Closed-ended questions are good for getting a precise answer, but they tend to shut down a conversation. If you want to keep the conversation moving along, ask an open-ended question right after you get the answer to a closed-ended question.

There are two simple devices you can use to keep things moving. Use them when the conversation starts to slow down and you don't have a specific question to ask.

Ask, "Oh, really?" That usually will encourage the other person to continue with what they were saying. There are several variations on "Oh, really?" such as "Is that right?" and "Sounds interesting...." Mix and match and make up your own versions.

The other device is to repeat the last few words of what the other person just said. If they say they were "really excited," you can say, "Really excited?" If they say, "So I went to check the mail," you can say "To check the mail?"

USE SILENCE EFFECTIVELY

I've learned that I do best when I wait for silence before forming the next question or comment. When I do that, I find myself attuned to what is being communicated to me. I don't even think about what I should say next, until I have listened to what is being said, and then process what I should say next during silence.

Allowing everyone to think during silence promotes discovery more than just jumping in with whatever question or comment comes to mind. If you wait and concentrate on what you've heard, you're more likely to say something relevant and helpful. Getting comfortable with silence and using it properly will help you build relationships as well as trust.

Silence is:

» The source of acknowledgement,
» The presence of appreciation, and
» The genesis of connecting one with another.

Fight the urge to fill silence with conversation. Don't automatically lead with your own ideas. Instead, embrace the silence and be curious.

Most Americans get uncomfortable when silence stretches on for more than a few seconds. Your conversation partner may be one of those people who need to jump right in and fill the silence. Allow it. Or, he or she may be much more comfortable with long silence than you are. You should practice being silent for longer stretches to handle those situations.

Here are some other tips and practices I have found helpful in my journey to improve my listening skills; they may help you, too:

» Pray for help and guidance to focus on the individual you are listening to.
» Make a conscious effort to clear out your thoughts before starting a discussion.
» Wait for silence before formulating the next question or comment.

» Reserve judgment.
» Strive to be more interested than interesting.

I challenge you to assess your current listening skills and commit yourself to improving in this area. I will guarantee it will make you a better leader and a better person.

In the last chapter I said that a key aspect of building relationships is to be present in people's lives. When you are present, and listening effectively, you will find yourself in situations where you can help people deal with real-life issues.

Being a great listener and empathetic to the needs of others gets at the essence of servant leadership, which would say that true leadership emerges from those whose primary motivation is a deep desire to help others.

EXERCISE

Monitor your next few conversations. Before the conversation, remind yourself how you want to act. During the conversation, move the amount of time you are talking to around 20 percent of the conversation, to enhance your abilities as a listener. Ask good questions. Use silence to make the conversation better. After the conversation, review your performance and think about what to do differently next time.

PLAYING TO THEIR STRENGTHS

For just as each of us has one body with many members, and these members do not all have the same function, so in Christ we, though many, form one body, and each member belongs to all the others. We have different gifts, according to the grace given to each of us.
~ Romans 12:4–6

My gift is building environments that foster high performance through the development of a culture of servant leadership. To help me, God has given me mentors, personal attributes, and a heart for learning. But I am not a creative person, or visionary by nature. Therefore, I know I need to get creative, visionary people on my team so my weakness doesn't drag the team down. That's part of what teamwork is all about.

LEARNING FROM HOCKEY

I grew up in Illinois before hockey gained the national popularity it enjoys today, so I didn't become a hockey fan until we moved to Minnesota, "The State of Hockey." We moved here when my sons were four and two years old. They grew up in that hockey culture, and the game became a huge part of our lives.

Both our sons fell in love with this great game and played hockey for many years. So we've had to learn a lot about hockey. Hockey is truly a team sport.

I feel one of the greatest lessons hockey teaches a servant leader is the importance of capitalizing on people's strengths. On a hockey team, everyone has a specific role to play. Some players are great scorers, others great playmakers, some are fantastic defensive players, and others physical agitators. As Paul said, "We have different gifts." Putting people in positions where they can play to their strengths makes the team better.

There's another benefit, too. Putting people in roles where they can use their strengths and passion builds their self-esteem. And that sets up a powerful cycle of personal growth, willingness to take risks, and concentrating on getting the job done. In the end, that leads to great results.

Sam Walton once said, "Outstanding leaders go out of their way to boost the self-esteem of their personnel. If people believe in themselves, it is amazing what they can accomplish."

That's easy to say and hard to do. It sounds great in theory, but how do you go about doing it?

Search for the term "finding strengths" on Google and you'll get more than fifty million results. Many of them offer great tools you can use to help people discover their strengths. Those tools are certainly helpful, but I feel most individuals already have a good understanding of their own strengths and weaknesses.

STRENGTHS AND WEAKNESSES

The real problem is that people work to hide their weaknesses. It's the result of a business culture that has specialized in catching people doing things wrong. People think their weaknesses are flaws that will keep them from getting that next raise or promotion.

Maybe that's true in some places. But servant leaders know the keys to success are to find the true strengths of each individual and put them in the right position to succeed.

This is only part of the challenge, though. We all have strengths, and we also have weaknesses. That's how God made us. We have to create a culture where weakness is okay. Start with yourself.

I believe a lot of my success has been due to understanding my strengths and my weaknesses. That's important, but it isn't enough.

You have to communicate with your team about your strengths and weaknesses and how you deal with them. It is imperative to talk openly about both strengths and weaknesses, and it has to start with you. The discussion with your team could look something like this.

» **Identify your strengths**. My top strength is creating a values-based culture and building high performing teams. I love getting the best out of the collective talents of the group and doing everything in my power to help each individual succeed.

» **Identify your weaknesses.** My creative and visionary skills are very weak. Ask me to create a vision for the future on my own, and I will sit idle and paralyzed for hours, staring off into space.

» **When you share your own weaknesses, you demonstrate to people that it's okay to have weaknesses.** God gave us different strengths and created us all with weaknesses.

» **Demonstrate that power is perfected in weakness.** To know your weaknesses is actually a strength. That's not just a bit of slick language. When you know your weaknesses, you can make them irrelevant and make the team stronger, too.

When I was president of the Banta Catalog Group, I knew we needed more of a visionary, somebody who could really look out and understand market dynamics. Because I was weak in that area, we went out and found a top-of-the-line vice president of marketing to help drive the vision of our organization.

I got her from a totally different world. Her name was Rochelle Shirk, and she had worked at the executive level at Dairy Queen and Buffet Foods. She was a valuable teammate and resource. She made our team better by bringing skills we didn't have. Another benefit was that, with Rochelle on board, other team members, including me, were freed to do more of the things we did well and had a passion for.

MAKING IT WORK

We could not have made that team stronger unless I, as a servant leader, did two things. First I had to be willing to admit my own weaknesses. Then I had to bring on someone who was strong where I was weak. There are three steps to making this work.

Help people identify their strengths and passions. If people can use their strengths and passions at work, they're more likely to be effective and engaged. Build on their strengths.

Help people identify their weaknesses and determine how to deal with them. The strategy is to make those weaknesses irrelevant. Determine if the weakness is getting in the way of top performance. If it is, you have two choices. You can assign the work to other people who have the right strengths. Or you can provide training and coaching to help the person with the weakness get "good enough." A person might have a weakness that isn't hurting them today, but that might keep them from achieving their personal goals. That's another case where you can provide training and coaching.

Commit publicly to building on people's strengths and making their weaknesses irrelevant. Building on the diversity of skills, strengths, and personalities on your team reinforces the fact that every individual is unique and can make an important contribution to the team. That will drive their engagement toward achieving the purpose and vision of the organization. One of my clients does this in a unique way. They identify every person's strengths using Gallup's Strength Finder. Everyone at the company has a plaque in their office that identifies their strengths, and they regularly discuss how to build on people's unique strengths. You don't need a plaque, though it's nice touch. You do need to identify everyone's strengths and weaknesses. Then build on those strengths while you make the weaknesses irrelevant.

EXERCISE

Set aside some time to have a specific discussion with members of your team on their strengths and weaknesses. Talk collectively on how you can most effectively capitalize on their strengths.

TRAINING AND COACHING

*And let us consider how we may spur one another
on toward love and good deeds, not giving up meeting
together, as some are in the habit of doing, but
encouraging one another—and all the more as
you see the Day approaching.*
~ Hebrews 10:24–25

I have had some great coaches as leaders over the years. Two of my favorites were Jack Ashelman and Ron Musil. They were very different personalities, but each of them recognized potential in me and both took a Coach Approach to allow me to develop my leadership skills and competency.

They left me free to run my businesses, but they were always there to ask challenging questions, push performance to new levels, and support me. They gave me encouragement and recognition when it was warranted.

It's important to remember that I was just a kid, really. I was still in my twenties when Jack hired me. A lot of bosses would have been coming around every day to check on me and make sure I was doing things right. Not Jack. He trusted me, and that made a huge difference in my confidence and the way I learned to lead. I learned a lot about the power of trust from Jack.

Ron was my boss after I'd proven that I was trustworthy. He broadened my horizons and deepened my skills by sending me to the Carlson School of Business. He was also a strong people person, and I learned a lot about building a dream team from him.

I learned a lot from both men about the importance of one-on-one discussions, how to assess a person's abilities, and how to be an effective leader. Jack and Ron were wise leaders who gave me help, respect, and support, while constantly pushing me to improve. They showed the way by what they said and how they acted. Without them, I would not be the leader I am today.

THE DIFFERENCE BETWEEN TRAINING AND COACHING

A key aspect of building relationships with the people you serve is to be an effective coach and mentor for them. Training is a key way to improve their skills. Here are a few key distinctions between training and coaching:

Training	Coaching
About the coach	About the person being coached
Telling	Asking
Advising	Drawing out
Solving	Promoting discovery
Directing	Supporting
Can foster dependency	Can foster self-reliance

When you as a leader are in the *training* mode, you are providing information and knowledge. When in a *coaching* mode, you come with the belief that the person being coached has the knowledge and ability within them, and it is your role to promote discovery and bring out the best of the individual.

People want to work for leaders who recognize the level of interaction and guidance that they need when performing their responsibilities and who are there to help. It is absolutely critical that you make an accurate assessment of both a person's passion and competence around their tasks to know the level of your interaction that they need and whether training or coaching is appropriate.

WHEN TO TRAIN AND WHEN TO COACH

There is an appropriate time for training and an appropriate time for coaching. Proper assessment of the right time for each activity will provide true value for the people you are working with.

Training is appropriate when

» People are new in their job or role and need information, knowledge, and skills to do their job
» A new, unfamiliar system or process has been introduced into the company or their department

Coaching is appropriate when

» You have willing participants who have goals they want to achieve
» The goals for the people being coached are self-development and self-reliance

When you do it right, several good things happen. Your people get better at their work and move toward achieving their God-given potential. That's better for them and for the team. And your relationship with your team improves as they witness you helping team members grow and develop. Servant leaders are intentional about stepping into the applicable role to advance the ability and skills of the people that they serve.

EXERCISE

Consider each of the people on your team. For each one, identify one area where they could benefit from coaching and one area where training would improve their performance.

POSITIVE ATTITUDE

*May the God of hope fill you with all joy and peace, as
you trust in him, so that you may overflow with hope by
the power of the Holy Spirit.*
~ Romans 15:13

I once had a boss who felt it was his job to always point out the negative. When he went on a plant tour, it was to find things that weren't going right and point them out. Nobody really ever wanted to see him or talk to him. He didn't have any true relationships with people. He even sat in his office until all hours of the night, just so that he could say he was there longer than anyone else.

I hated going on plant tours with that man. You could feel the energy and friendliness drain out of the place as he walked around pointing out things that weren't just right and directing others to fix them. He didn't act at all like the boss I had before.

That prior boss was Gary Hamacher. He was the vice president and general manager of the plant in Pontiac, Illinois. He's the man who gave me the opportunity to be customer service manager and later production control manager. Gary was my first great leadership role model after my father. Looking back, I'm really glad he was my boss before I worked for "Mr. Negative."

Because of Gary, I knew that what Mr. Negative was doing not only made people uncomfortable but demonstrated terrible leadership. I have found that if you consistently show up with a positive attitude, it improves the environment for people.

The Power of Positive Attitude

When people see the leader with a positive attitude, it leads to better relationships and better performance. I've also found that thinking about Romans 15:13 helps me keep a positive attitude, lift people up, and build relationships to another level.

People don't want to follow leaders who are always looking at the glass half empty. They appreciate a leader who is optimistic and smiling and provides hope for a positive future.

Look Out the Windshield, Not in the Rearview Mirror

An important part of having a positive attitude is your ability to look out the windshield instead of the rearview mirror as you go through life. Times are not always going to be good. There will be struggles along the way. God promises that in Scripture.

However, we have the choice to make the best of every situation and look forward and lead towards a better future. The past can provide perspective; but if we look only at the past, we won't see the present clearly or look forward to a better future. If you drive a car while constantly looking in the rearview mirror, you will eventually crash.

Servant leaders expand the windshield and diminish the rearview mirror. They see the best future in even the most challenging of situations. They don't try to hide the past, they don't try to blame others, and they don't punish themselves for things gone bad. Sure, they take responsibility and learn from the past, but their focus is on building a better future.

You will build relationships and trust when you

- » Smile
- » Focus first on the positive
- » Provide optimism in the face of uncertainty
- » Provide hope in the midst of challenges
- » Believe in people and how they can respond in tough times

After I wrote the first draft of this chapter, I was talking with my friend, Wally Bock. He told me about one of his mother's sayings that's just spot on. Whenever something went wrong, she would ask, "What good can we make of this?" That's a great question to help you keep looking out the windshield.

When you are seen as someone who consistently provides hope for a better future, you are a leader people want to align with. Here are some ways you can be intentional about looking forward and providing hope.

- » Accept—there is no better way to give a person hope than by accepting them for who they are, not what they do.
- » Love—truly care for people.
- » Appreciate—say thank you.
- » Praise achievements, effort, and progress.
- » Show compassion.
- » Encourage—urge people to hang in during tough times, and persist in achieving their goals.
- » Help people "make something good of this."
- » Show people they're important by spending time with them and listening.
- » Protect—ensure a "no fear" atmosphere.
- » Support—walk alongside people; be there for them.

EXERCISE

Commit to yourself to smiling more. Set a timer on your phone on an hourly basis for one week, to remind yourself to smile. Check the impact that this one small behavior shift makes in your personal attitude and in the attitude of those around you.

YOUR LEADERSHIP PORTRAIT

*Therfore each of you must put off falsehood
and speak truthfully to your neighbor, for we are
all members of one body.*
~ Ephesians 4:25

This year was the 30-year anniversary of my father-in-law's getting killed in a bicycle accident. He had worked hard his whole life and he was looking forward to his retirement, which was just three months away.

Kim and I had just finished dinner when we got the call. I remember all the details of that call: what we were wearing, where we were in the room, and what we had for dinner. We've never had that meal again.

My father-in-law's death had a significant impact on me. It created some deep and powerful memories, and it taught me several lessons. Here are a few things I learned.

I learned to keep my priorities straight. Family events and relationships are more important than anything going on at work.

I learned to keep things in perspective. Most things are not life-or-death situations.

I learned to cherish every moment God provides me on this earth and to use those moments to be intentional about adding value to people. Servant leaders know that God placed us here for each other.

My father-in-law's death shaped my leadership style. Whenever someone who worked for me was working late on a night when one of his or her kids had a game or a school event, I'd push that person out the door. I was able to stay calm when others might be treating a business problem like it was a life-or-death situation. And his death really deepened my understanding of what it means to be a servant leader.

We all have things in our past that influence how we act and how we lead. Futurists call those "perception-shaping events." We all have people who have shown us the way and mentored us and shaped our leadership style. Think about the people you put on your Leadership Mount Rushmore.

Do the people within your sphere of influence know and understand your past and what has brought you to this point? I have found that sharing your Leadership Portrait is an extremely powerful tool for a leader to build relationships and enhance influence. Servant leaders are transparent!

WHAT IS A LEADERSHIP PORTRAIT?

A good portrait painter or photographer wants to capture more than the likeness of his or her subject. The artist includes details that tell you something about the person's character or achievement. Your Leadership Portrait should do the same thing.

Your Leadership Portrait should include events and people that have impacted you and your life. They're the things that have made you who you are today. Include your background, who and what has shaped your development as a leader, your purpose, your values, and your vision for your future, as well as your leadership philosophy. Here is a list of questions to ask yourself.

» Who are key mentors in my life that had an impact on my leadership philosophy?
» What are some events in my life that have shaped my leadership philosophy?
» What is my personal purpose?
» What are my core values?
» What is my vision for the key responsibility areas of my life?
» What are my beliefs about leading?

You've already done some important work on your Leadership Portrait. Now is the time to bring some of that work together. Putting in the work to develop your Leadership Portrait will yield solid benefits.

WHY YOU WANT TO DEVELOP YOUR LEADERSHIP PORTRAIT

There is a lot of power in this process. From a personal standpoint, it clarifies and provides direction for both your short-term and long-term decisions and actions. A clear purpose, values, and vision will guide you on your journey and provide direction. They will remind you of what's important and the kind of person you want to be.

One of the most powerful components of your Leadership Portrait is your background and mentors who have brought you to this point in your leadership journey. My father was my lifetime leadership mentor. He passed away a few years ago, but the example he set will always be the foundation for the way I lead. Here are a few of the lessons I learned from my dad about servant leadership.

I learned the importance of **humility**. He was the humblest of men, never looking to bring attention to himself but instead always working behind the scenes on behalf of his family and co-workers.

I learned the importance of **hard work** and a **commitment to excellence**. In the printing business, there were always deadlines to meet, and he never called it a day until the work was done and at the highest level of quality.

I learned the importance of **selflessness**. Even though Dad was always busy with his job, yardwork, or general work around the house, he always had time for me when I wanted it. He would spend countless hours catching me while I pitched to him in the summer, playing Ping-Pong with me in the winter, or talking "shop" as I learned the printing trade.

I learned the importance of **commitment to core values**. There was never any question in our household that everything we had was a gift of God. It was up to us to be good stewards of what we had been given. And when he drew a line in the sand, I knew not to cross it or there would be consequences.

I learned the importance of **positive recognition**. After any sporting event I participated in, my dad always made a positive comment about some aspect of the game; he always found a way to build me up. That carried on into my working years as well. My dad was my biggest cheerleader.

I learned the importance of **mutual respect and trust**. Dad had a huge amount of respect for all people in the organization, no matter what their role. I never forget that.

As you craft your Leadership Portrait, you will reflect on the mentors who had a significant impact in your life. I was fortunate to have the opportunity to thank my dad for everything before he passed away. I urge you take the time to give your mentors a gift by thanking them for what they have done for you.

Don't assume they know you're grateful. Be intentional about letting them know specifically about the positive impact that they had on you. Leaders whom I have encouraged to thank their mentors have told me that it had a profound impact on the person who has mentored them.

Knowing and understanding the way people have mentored you throughout your life and career can also help you pay that forward to people you have a chance to mentor in your life. Sharing your story with others will absolutely help build relationships with people.

Let down your guard and show the real person you are. It will be freeing and will enable you to not have to check which door you are going through to know how to act. You can be the same person wherever you are.

Bring people into closer relationship with you, as they understand you better. It will lead to high performance in all aspects of your life.

After you've created your Leadership Portrait, you'll find it easier to verbalize what is important to you and why it is important. It will deepen your resolve to live a life of meaning. As powerful as those benefits are, your Leadership Portrait will have even more impact on your life as a leader if you share it with others.

WHY YOU WANT TO SHARE YOUR LEADERSHIP PORTRAIT

When you share your Leadership Portrait, you allow your people to see you as a real person. That will break down barriers, create an atmosphere of freedom, and reduce fear. It will enhance the relationships you have with your people. That's being truly transparent, and being transparent is powerful!

In my experience, when leaders become transparent and share their Leadership Portrait, many powerful things take place between the parties involved. Here are some:

- » Deeper relationships
- » Clarity
- » Emotion
- » Understanding
- » Vulnerability
- » Empathy

All these things are components that will drive relationships to another level.

HOW TO SHARE YOUR LEADERSHIP PORTRAIT

When you share your Leadership Portrait, you strengthen your relationship with others. There are three ways you can share.

Share your Leadership Portrait in normal conversation. The easiest way to share your Leadership Portrait is simply to make sharing part of the conversations that occur naturally during the day. That's powerful, because it lets you share the pieces of your portrait that are relevant to a specific situation and a specific person. When you share those pieces of your life, you make yourself vulnerable and transparent and deepen your relationship with the person you're talking with.

That's a good start. But I encourage you to go further and share your Leadership Portrait with your team and those you lead.

Share your Leadership Portrait with the people who work with you.
Sit down with your team or stand up at an all-employee meeting and
share your Leadership Portrait. This is an opportunity to talk through
your portrait and give people a deep sense of who you are and why you
act the way you do.

Whenever I was re-assigned and started working with a new team, I
shared my Leadership Portrait with them. The first time I did it, it felt like
a huge risk, but it worked so well that I've done it ever since.

Anytime I'd get a new direct report, I would do the same thing. Right
up front they learned who they were working for, what my background
was, and what it was going to be like to work for me.

Ask everyone on your team to share. The most powerful way to use Leadership Portraits is when everyone shares. When I work with organizations
to improve their culture, I set up and facilitate a session where the entire
senior leadership team has a Leadership Portrait sharing time.

I recently had the opportunity to listen to a number of people share
their Leadership Portrait with a group of peers within their organization.
The power of this process never ceases to amaze me. In this session, people who had worked together for more than twenty-five years found out
things they had never known about each other. You could feel the close-
ness of the relationships in the room build as they each shared their Portrait. This high-performing organization became even stronger, because
they were intentional about this process.

You don't want to order people to share, coerce them into sharing, or
shame them into it. That's not servant leadership, and it poisons relationships. But if you lead the way and allow people to decide when and if
they're ready, group sharing can work. Here's how it usually goes.

I suggest that you model the behavior first by sharing your Leadership
Portrait with your team. Then explain what goes into a Leadership Portrait and set up another session where people can share with each other.

When you have that second session, not everyone will have thought
through their personal Leadership Portrait. Some people will be uncom-

fortable sharing. Don't worry. Things will work out. Just encourage people to share, make it safe, and then watch good things happen.

I recently worked with a group where one senior leader thought this was all touchy-feely nonsense. He didn't do any preparation for our sharing session, and I'm pretty sure he planned on not sharing anything personal. And he didn't, for most of the session.

But the comfort level of the other people and the way they participated affected him. As we were nearing the end of the session, he began sharing. It was just off-the-cuff, very unprepared; but it was extremely powerful. He shared things that people who had worked with him for years didn't know anything about. There were tears in many eyes. You could feel the people in the room growing closer together.

We have spent this entire section reviewing the importance of being intentional about building relationships. One of the best ways to develop an environment of trust that will enable relationships to flourish is for you as the leader to openly share your Leadership Portrait.

EXERCISE

» Block out the time and develop your personal Leadership Portrait.

» Commit to sharing your Leadership Portrait with your team.

LEADING JESUS' WAY TO BUILD RELATIONSHIPS

One of the teachers of the law came and heard them debating. Noticing that Jesus had given them a good answer, he asked him, "Of all the commandments, which is the most important?"

"The most important one," answered Jesus, "is this: 'Hear, O Israel: The Lord our God, the Lord is one. Love the Lord your God with all your heart and with all your soul and with all your mind and with all your strength.' The second is this: 'Love your neighbor as yourself.' There is no commandment greater than these."
~ Mark 12:28–31

God clearly considers relationships sacred, and as precious as the individuals who form them. Consider the following facts from Scripture.

» Six of the Ten Commandments address our relationships with people, while four direct our relationship with God. (Exodus 20)
» Jesus makes peaceful human relationships a prerequisite for worship. (Matthew 5:23)

» Jesus makes relationships a prerequisite for receiving God's forgiveness. (Matthew 6:15 & Matthew 18)
» Jesus makes relationships a prerequisite for answered prayer. (Matthew 18:19)
» Harmonious relationships are key to welcoming God's presence. (Matthew 18:20)

The entire New Testament is about relationship reconciliation. Getting along with others is a common human challenge, even for followers of Jesus. In the preceding passage from Mark, Jesus further clarifies the importance of relationships as He describes the two most important commands.

Jesus makes it crystal clear: We are to love God and love people. There is no greater calling, no greater purpose, no more significant investment of our time, talents, energies, and resources than to develop relationships by loving God and others. Therefore, servant leadership can be grounded *only* in the worldview that sees every human as created in God's image, and love at that level (Genesis 1:26).

Jesus clearly believed in the power of relationships. Let's look at a time that He went out of His way to act with love and build a relationship. In Mark 1:40–42, we find the story about Jesus and the leper.

> A man with leprosy came to him and begged him on his knees, "If you are willing, you can make me clean." Moved with compassion Jesus reached out his hand and touched the man. "I am willing," he said. "Be clean!" Immediately the leprosy left him and he was cleansed.

Let's break this down a bit:

"A man with leprosy came to him…"

Jesus was approachable, and welcomed a man who had no legal right to come close.

"… and begged him on his knees."

Jesus not only let him approach, He let him impose a request.

"If you are willing, you can make me clean."

Jesus was not offended by the man's incomplete understanding of his character.

"Moved with compassion…"

Jesus engaged emotionally.

"Jesus reached out his hand and touched the man."

Jesus "touched" the man. The onlookers must have been shocked, because by touching the leper Jesus was taking a huge risk. Jesus could cleanse the man of leprosy without touching him, but Jesus chose a deeper connection than that.

"'I am willing,' he said."

Jesus corrected the man's partial understanding of His compassion.

"'Be clean!' Immediately the leprosy left him and he was cleansed."

Jesus enforced His touch with a command. Two words, and the deal was done!

Jesus healed this leper through touch, because leprosy had eaten away more than his flesh. It had robbed him of relationship. Jesus healed him *through* intimacy and *for* it. Jesus does the same today. He saves us *through* and *for* relationship.

Here are some lessons we can learn from Jesus about valuing relationships:

- » Be approachable.
- » Entertain requests.
- » Take no offense.
- » Engage emotionally.
- » Meet the deepest need.
- » Reveal your true character.
- » Give the gift of communication.

Building relationships is the most important daily work you can do as a leader. Connect with people throughout your day, and act intentionally to improve the relationship with every encounter. The more time and effort you put in this area, the more effective you will be as a servant leader.

Servant leadership is all about thinking first and foremost about the greater good of other people. That won't happen if you aren't focusing on building relationships on a consistent basis.

As in the other areas of importance, this comes naturally for some and is more challenging for others. But there is no excuse for not concentrating on building relationships. After all, it is a command from God.

Look for situations where you can make improvement on building relationships. You might want to do a better job of illustrating mutual respect and trust. Maybe you will want to make a big effort to become a better listener or a better coach. Or you might want to focus on building on other people's strengths. Being intentional about always having a positive attitude and smile can go a long way in this regard. Sharing your Leadership Portrait with others can be a powerful relationship builder.

Every improvement will be a step in the right direction. People will notice, and they will want to be around you. It will expand your level of influence and allow you to have a significant positive impact on the world. Remember this is important in all aspects of your life.

EXERCISE

Study the following additional times where Jesus went out of His way to develop relationships. What can you learn from each one?

» Zacchaeus (Luke 19:1–10)

» Promiscuous woman (John 8:2–11)

» Criminal on the Cross (Luke 23:39–43)

» Saul/Paul (Acts 9:1–31)

BUILD
CHARACTER

INTRODUCTION

For the Lord sees not as man sees: man looks on the outward appearance, but the Lord looks on the heart.
~ 1 Samuel 16:7

Character is what flows out of the heart. Your character defines you as a leader. People want to follow people they can look up to and trust. Servant leaders are intentional about building character.

Personal character is the sum of all the qualities that define us as individuals and as leaders. Warren Bennis cited Harvard research that indicated as much as 85 percent of a leader's performance depends on his or her character. My experience in thirty-five years in business tells me the same thing.

The personal character of leaders defines their depth and stability, what they are truly made of. Character is a lot like the rocks I clear from the paths at our maple syrup operation.

I recently ran across a rock partially buried on one of the trails. For safety purposes I thought we should dig up the rock and remove it from the trail. I've moved a lot of those rocks over the years.

Normally what you see above the surface is about a quarter to a half of the rock. Based on that, I thought this rock would be easy to dig up and move, but I was wrong.

This particular rock turned out to be much more challenging. What I saw above ground was only about 10 percent of the rock. It had much more depth, stability, and balance than what met the eye. Servant leadership is similar.

When you look at leaders, you see many things. You can tell easily if they are intelligent, whether they have good technical skills, and how much they understand the business and the industry. What you don't see, because it is below the surface and in their heart, is their character. That's what Dwight Moody meant when he said, "Character is what you are in the dark."

The importance of character separates servant leaders from other leaders. Servant leaders know that people will follow them only if they are trusted; and they will trust their leaders based on their leaders' character.

Key aspects of a servant leader's heart that will separate him or her from the pack include:

> » A desire to serve others, above and beyond oneself
> » A desire for never-ending development of one's ability
> » A desire to achieve one's very best
> » A willingness to always accept responsibility for one's actions
> » A commitment to being humble and vulnerable
> » A desire to make a positive impact on society

Issues of the heart don't change overnight, but we can be intentional about positively developing all the areas of our character in an effort to become better servant leaders.

Servant leaders periodically check these areas to see how they are doing. They ask others (truth tellers) what they think. Servant leaders commit themselves to improving all areas of their character.

This process will make an impact on your level of influence and the significance of your work and life. In this section we'll review ways you can assess and develop your character.

EXERCISE

Before you turn to the next chapter in this section, identify someone whose character you admire. Then write down what that person says or does that you admire. Keep your description handy as you work through the next three chapters.

MODEL THE WAY

When he had finished washing their feet, he put on his clothes and returned to his place. "Do you understand what I have done for you?" he asked them.
~ John 13:12

Jesus practiced what He preached. He walked His talk every day. When He washed His disciples' feet, He demonstrated what true servant leadership is all about. That is how you build character. You model the way.

It's important to stay connected with all the people in your organization. You can't do that sitting in your office all day. When I was a senior leader, I committed to getting out and talking to people throughout the plant several times every day. This illustrated to all the other leaders in the organization how important that was to me. I modeled something I wanted them to do.

If I saw trash on the floor while I was walking around, I picked it up. If a press crew was dealing with an issue and I could help, I dug in and helped. I wanted other leaders in the organization to do those things, and my behavior modeled how I wanted them to act. My behavior sent the message about what I wanted.

Albert Schweitzer once said, "Example is not the *main* thing in influencing others, it is the *only* thing." This was certainly true with my father, who was one of my main mentors in my life. My father didn't tell me how to live; he lived, and he let me watch him do it. I learned a lot from watching him.

We touched on this in the chapter on values. You demonstrate what's really important to you by the way you act.

That's why it's vital to be fully aware of the message you are sending in the way you conduct yourself. You might be saying all the right things, but if your actions don't back up what you are saying, it won't matter much. People may doubt what their leaders say, but they usually believe what they do.

YOU ARE THE MODEL

As a leader, you are "on stage" every day. Your people watch every move you make. They take what you do as a model for what you want them to do.

A young woman at an Executive and Entrepreneurial Leadership Forum at Alexandria Technical College asked me the question that sums up the challenge. She asked me, "How do you keep servant leadership at the front of your mind and actions on a *daily* basis and consistently model the way?"

That young woman recognized the challenge we face in changing the human-nature aspect of self-centeredness, to a heart and passion for serving others. This is a true battle for all of us, and it takes a plan of intentionality to be a servant leader of high character. The really hard part is doing it all day, every day.

We are all different. So you may find that coaching is something you have to work hard at, to get it right. But perhaps you have no trouble maintaining a positive attitude. I guarantee you that another servant leader is having a hard time with that positive attitude, but finds that coaching comes naturally.

We do differ according to gifts given us. But we all have things that come easily and things we have to really work at if we are going to be the leader God wants us to be.

I don't know you, so I can't tell you the specifics of how to meet your personal challenges of being a servant leader. But I can tell you how things work for me, and for me it comes down to two words: *focus* and *commitment*.

START THE DAY RIGHT

I have to keep a *daily focus* on my personal purpose, values, and behaviors, and I have to *stay committed* to the behaviors I have outlined for my values. My personal values are:

» Spirituality
» Mutual respect and trust
» Commitment to excellence
» Well-being: body, mind, and spirit

These are some behaviors I have outlined for myself that help me in my quest to be a servant leader:

» I will spend the start of every morning in solitude and devotion, reading scripture and listening to what God has to say to me that day.
» Every day, I will look to encourage anyone I come into contact with.
» I will never be satisfied with the status quo and will always look for how I can improve the value I provide.
» I will take care of myself by exercising four days a week, and eating 2100 or fewer calories per day so I can feel good and serve others effectively.
» I will look for ways to get feedback on my performance to provide insights on where I need to improve.

I've found that I'm more likely to be the servant leader God wants me to be when I'm intentional about getting my mind right and reminding myself of how I want to act. That starts with my morning ritual.

Hyrum Smith wrote about the "magic fifteen minutes" you should take in the morning to plan your day. For me it's more like a magic forty-five minutes, where I'm really setting the course for the day by connecting with God, by listening to what He's got to say, and by asking for guidance in every interaction I'm going to have that day.

During the day I keep going back to God in prayer. Before each coaching call, any time I give a speech, before every client interaction, before whatever, I'm just asking for God to bring the words. I definitely have the prayer habit.

The challenge for me is to keep those values and behaviors in mind throughout the day. When I do that, I have a good day as a servant leader. When I don't, I often end the day wishing I had done better. I often fall short on demonstrating my values. Many times I've also let things happen when I should have spoken up.

A while back, I had a veteran of the Navy share with me something he learned from his captain on a submarine during a tour in the Pacific Ocean. He said it was one of the most important leadership lessons he learned while in the Navy:

> What you allow in your presence becomes the rule of your command.

Wow, did that ever hit home with me! I thought back to a situation from early in my leadership career when I had done that very thing.

When I was 26 years old, I was transferred and promoted to plant manager of a printing company in Milwaukee. My leadership team was a group of seasoned veterans in the industry.

I remember conducting my first few leadership team meetings and being struck by the amount of swearing that seemed to be commonplace and well accepted as part of the culture. I didn't like it.

This was not the culture I wanted to lead. I thought I would just model the way by never swearing. I figured the team would detect that I didn't talk like that, so it wasn't acceptable for others to talk that way either. Guess what? It never changed. People went right on swearing the way they did prior to my arrival. I never said anything about the swearing, and so it became okay, something I condoned.

It's not enough to just model the way. It's just as important to clearly and immediately address any issues that violate the values of the organization. When you allow unacceptable behaviors to go unaddressed, you send the message that the behavior is okay.

Servant leaders provide constructive criticism when necessary. They coach their team members on areas of performance and behaviors that need improvement. Sometimes that takes courage. I did not have that courage as a 26-year-old plant manager. I pray that I will have it if I need it today.

SERVANT LEADERS MAKE THEIR EXPECTATIONS CLEAR

One of the most important things you can do is set clear expectations. We've already talked about expectations, especially in the chapters on setting expectations for the organization and for yourself. Tell people what you expect, so they don't have to guess.

Go beyond simply stating your expectations. Make heroes out of people who are living and modeling the values. Tell the stories of what they did, and you send a message about what you expect.

Ask yourself: "Is there anything I am allowing that doesn't fit the culture I want?" Then pray for strength and wisdom and set about changing things.

MODELING THE WAY IS HARD WORK

I have also found that to consistently model the way, I need help. I need God's help, and I need people in my life who will push me to new levels of performance. Are you intentional about aligning yourself with people like that?

In his book, *The 15 Invaluable Laws of Growth*, John Maxwell wrote about the "Law of the Environment." This law illustrates the importance of surrounding yourself with high performers and with people who want to grow and who will challenge you.

That's one of the great things about our Servant Leadership Roundtable groups. The people who come and participate learn about servant leadership, but something more happens, too.

The roundtables become what psychologists call "reference groups." Your mother probably knew about them, even though she never used those words. She probably worried about who your friends were, because she knew that we tend to think about our behavior and values in comparison to the people we hang around with.

In the roundtables, people come in contact with others who value servant leadership and want to become faith-based servant leaders. You may not be part of one of our Servant Leadership Roundtables, but you will find your path easier if you spend time with other people who have servant leadership values. You may also want to consider working with a coach or mentor.

This has been critical to my growth over the years. Sometimes I have to intentionally elicit the help of these people. Other times I need to be aware of their presence, listen, and be open to their challenge.

Ten years ago I sought out the help of a coach from the Ken Blanchard Companies to help me learn the process of driving a purpose-driven, values-based culture. That decision to develop an ongoing coaching relationship with Chris Edmonds definitely helped me get to places that I would never have gotten to on my own.

My own family also pushes me to be my best. My younger son Dan is pushing me to be better, to be more connected in the world of social media, and to provide more relevant content on a more consistent basis. He has a servant heart that understands the needs of his generation and is providing insights on how to deliver for them.

Here are some things to consider when looking for ways to build your character and enhance your ability to model the way:

- » Seek out mentors.
- » Hire a coach.
- » Participate in leadership peer group or roundtable.
- » Seek out training opportunities.
- » Ask more questions.
- » Work on your listening skills.
- » Set aside time for daily reading.

When you improve your learning environment, you set yourself up to receive several benefits:

» You will see things in a different light.
» You will discover you have more within you.
» You will enhance your level of influence.
» You will become a better leader, mentor, and coach.

I feel very fortunate to have many people in my life who care enough to push me to new levels of performance. I learn a lot from my wife and both my sons when I listen. I also learn from my coaches, clients, and peers. I'm grateful to all of them for being willing to invest in me.

James W. Ayers was a Marine captain who was killed in action in Vietnam. Today, decades later, men who served with him tell stories about what an exceptional leader he was. One of his mantras is perfect here:

There is no leadership without leadership by example.

EXERCISE

These four questions are a self-examination. Answer them and determine what you need to do to improve things.

» How do you start your day? Do you spend a magic fifteen minutes or longer, planning your day and preparing to make it a good one?

» If you were in a silent film, would the people who watched you be able to tell what your values are?

» Is there anything you have tacitly approved because you allowed it, that needs to be changed?

» Do you surround yourself with people who will inspire you, teach you, support you, and push you?

DEVELOPING TRUST

---

*But I am like an olive tree flourishing in the house of
God; I trust in God's unfailing love for ever and ever.*
~ Psalm 52:8

We know that we can trust in God's love. We also want to follow leaders here on earth whom we can trust. The people on your team crave a leader they can trust. Without trust you may get compliance, but you will never get commitment.

In 1987 I left the company I had worked for from the start of my career and joined the Banta Corporation. It was a big move, both psychologically and geographically.

We would have to move our family from the big city of Milwaukee to Long Prairie, Minnesota, a small town in what I thought of as the northern edge of the country. In fact, Long Prairie is closer to Winnipeg in Canada than it is to Milwaukee.

I was willing to move my family and take on the challenging work that awaited me in Long Prairie because I trusted Jack Ashelman, the man who recruited me and who would be my boss. Jack and Ron Musil, who became my boss later, lived up to every commitment they ever made to me. They were people of high integrity whom I could trust. It's no wonder they built such high-performing teams.

I talked earlier in the book about leadership being influence. In my experience, if there is a lack of trust, influence will be significantly inhibited in any relationship. Don't leave this to chance. Leaders of high character are intentional about building trust.

DRIVE OUT FEAR

Fear is the opposite of trust. When people worry about what will happen to them or whether their leader has their best interests at heart, they spend their time thinking about protecting themselves instead of doing a great job. Fear destroys high performance, innovation, and growth. When fear is part of your culture, you have to drive it out so those good things can happen. I witnessed that process happen with a client in a large organization.

The president of the company had learned some servant leadership principles, so he had an idea of what a high-performing culture of trust looked like. He knew his company didn't have the culture he wanted, but he also knew that he was part of the problem. Here's what he did to start the change rolling.

The president brought his thirty-five top leaders together offsite. He gave each one of them a green card and a red card. After an introduction where he shared some fairly positive statistics on their business, he said that he wanted to know how satisfied they were with the culture of the company.

He asked them to hold up the red card if they were unsatisfied and the green card if they were satisfied. Everyone was to hold up their card at the same time, so they couldn't influence each other.

Only three people held up a red card. The other thirty-two held up green cards, indicating that they thought the culture was okay. That was not what the president had expected.

He knew people weren't happy with the current culture, and he recognized that there was so much fear in the room that many of his top leaders were unwilling to risk telling the truth. So he told the group two things.

He said he wasn't happy with the current culture and that he was taking the responsibility for its current state. Then he shared an overview of the servant leadership culture that he had a desire to build, and asked them for their support in helping to build it. Near the end of the meeting they took another vote. This time every card was red, but the leaders were committed to changing their culture.

That was a monumental day in the history of that organization. It was the start of a positive change in their culture and in the way they did business. They continue to improve every day.

The change started when the president acted courageously. He told his team that he thought the culture should be fixed, but he also took responsibility for it's being the way it was. He put himself in a weak spot so he could become stronger as a leader, and the company could become stronger as an organization.

In 2 Corinthians 12:9, the Apostle Paul said, "For when I am weak, then I am strong." That's often where positive change starts, especially when we're talking about trust issues.

WEAKNESS IS A STRENGTH

I was fortunate when I was promoted to head that customer service team in Pontiac. I was fortunate to realize how much I didn't know and how much my team members knew. I was fortunate to realize how much I had to learn and grow.

You won't improve if you think you've got it figured out and there isn't much to learn. When you have an attitude like that, it sends a message to your team that you already know it all so all they need to do is what you tell them. That's the fast route to a fear-based organization.

The great servant leaders I have known and read about all had an unending desire for improvement in these areas of character. They sought out coaches, mentors, peer groups, teachers, books, and every other opportunity to help them improve.

Those servant leaders also praised the people around them and encouraged them in every way possible. They provided opportunities for increased responsibility and autonomy when appropriate.

You must maintain the attitude that you will never fully arrive when it comes to character. Building character is a never-ending process of small consistent steps to become the leader that you want to be. Character isn't developed overnight; it takes time and attention and effort.

A SYSTEM OF LEADERSHIP

People value predictability and consistency in leaders. They want to know what to expect when they come to work. I found one way to ensure consistency for the people you are serving is to develop a system of leadership. This defines the cadence of your days, weeks, and months. The following was my system of leadership when I was running a business:

» Senior Leadership Team Meeting every Monday at 9:00 a.m.
» Walk through the plant twice a day to interact with employees
» Monthly financial review with the Senior Leadership Team
» Quarterly all-employee meetings on each shift
» Travel one week per month for customer visits
» One-on-one meetings with my direct reports every two weeks
» "Fireside Chat" with a different random group of employees every month
» Review key metrics every day

Your system will probably have some very different items. No matter what's on the list, your system should establish a regular cadence for your business so that people know what to expect when they come to work. But that's only part of your challenge.

When you're the leader, people should know what to expect from you. Here are a few things that make a servant leader predictable:

» Living out the organization's purpose, values, and vision
» Holding yourself and others to high standards
» Showing up for all your scheduled meetings and appointments
» Returning phone calls and emails promptly
» Being available when you are needed
» Finishing projects

» Seeking advice, counsel, and feedback from others
» Admitting mistakes and making them right

This consistency provides a model for other leaders to follow. It allows employees and customers to accurately predict and understand your reaction and availability. This is especially important, because the times you don't deliver will stand out in people's minds.

Psychologist Roy Baumeister has shown that human beings have a tendency to remember the times we were disappointed or hurt, more than the times we weren't. He calls it the "bad is stronger than good" effect. It means that you can keep every appointment for years, but people will remember the one time you missed an appointment without advance notice. It may not be fair, but it's the way we're made.

The good news is that keeping commitments is not about willpower. Instead, it is about developing a process to ensure delivery on commitments. I have found the following to be effective components of a process for consistently delivering on your commitments.

» **Make commitments that are in alignment with your purpose, values, and vision.** Doing so will ensure that you are passionate about the commitment and have a true internal desire to deliver.

» **Only make commitments you're sure you can deliver on.** Don't set yourself up for failure from the start. Be reasonable with yourself on what is humanly possible, given your schedule, capacity, and competence. Learning to say "No" when appropriate is a necessary part of the process of keeping commitments.

» **Document your commitments in writing.** Capture the commitment, who you committed it to, when you made the commitment, and when it is due. Capturing your commitments and tracking their progress in written form will ensure you stay abreast of what you need to accomplish on a daily, weekly, and monthly basis.

» **Share your commitments with an accountability partner.** Asking someone to come alongside you and hold you accountable for delivering on a commitment increases your odds of delivery. It also illustrates your vulnerability and need for help, which is an outstanding model of a servant leader.

» **Put your commitments into your calendar.** If you are like me, you are dependent on your calendar. Putting commitments into your calendar will discourage you from scheduling things that would prohibit you from delivering on your commitments. A few years ago I made a commitment to my wife to sit down with her daily after our workday and connect on how our day went. It is in my calendar every day at 5:00 p.m. as "Kim Time."

» **Know who depends on you and why it is important.** When you have intimate knowledge of who is depending on you to deliver, and what difference the successful completion of the commitment will have, it will provide extra passion for completion. You don't want to let people down.

The bottom line is that servant leaders aren't blown with the wind. They are more like a rock, someone who is predictable and whom people can count on in all situations. That builds trust and eliminates fear.

BE PRESENT AND APPROACHABLE

Leaders also build trust by being present and approachable to the people they are serving. Duke men's basketball coach Mike Krzyzewski said it well:

> How does a person show respect for anything? He gives it time. If you respect your children, you give them time. If you respect your employees, you listen to them. You give them time.

When I was in a corporate leadership role, that was the idea behind walking the plant twice a day and having conversations with the people I met there. It was why I had regular one-on-ones with my direct reports. It's why I still put "Kim Time" on my calendar.

Servant leaders recognize that they must build trust within their team. They also realize their personal character will drive that trust. Focus on being vulnerable, recognizing your weaknesses, and building others up. Develop a system of leadership for yourself. Be present and approachable with the people you meet. Collectively, all these things will enhance your personal character and build trust within your team.

EXERCISE

» Make some notes about your team's culture. What do you like? What do you want to change? Have some conversations with team members about the culture.

» Are there any areas of your performance where you've stopped improving? Should you change that?

» Do you have a system of leadership that sets the cadence for the days and weeks and months, so that people know what to expect?

» Do people feel safe bringing you good ideas or bad news?

CLIMATE SURVEY

And no creature is hidden from his sight, but all are naked and exposed to the eyes of him to whom we must give account.
~ Hebrews 4:13

Maybe "naked" is a bit much, but we do need to be exposed and vulnerable to the people we serve. We need to be open to feedback on how we can improve. And we need to set the example for openness and continual improvement. Climate surveys are a good way to do those things.

I'm not talking about the long, formal surveys that many companies conduct to measure engagement or morale, although those are important. The company I worked for conducted those surveys every year, and we learned a lot from them. But what I'm talking about in this chapter is a simpler climate survey that you conduct with your direct reports.

I recently completed climate surveys with all my coaching clients. I wanted to find out how I could improve in the service I provide them as their coach. That's one of the reasons you should do a climate survey: so you can find out things that people may not tell you in the everyday course of work.

The one common piece of feedback I received was they wanted me to be more diligent in holding them accountable. We end each coaching session with action items, and they asked me to be tougher on ensuring that they complete their commitments.

Accountability within a culture is vital. Without it the environment can be chaotic, because no one can count on anyone else. Without accountability you will never achieve a high-performing team or organization.

Accountability won't work if it's a one-way street. If I want accountability from others, I must first become accountable to them. That's how to generate mutual accountability.

Mutual accountability starts with leaders. When you set the example by being accountable, other people will follow your lead. Start by making sure the following are crystal clear.

» **Purpose, values, and vision**—people need to know where they are going and, most importantly, why they are going there. They also need to understand how they are supposed to behave on the journey.

» **Expectations**—what specifically are you expecting from the people in your sphere of influence? If you don't tell them, they will guess, and they might guess some things that you don't want. Goals should be very well defined, with specific completion dates.

» **Measurement and feedback**—keeping score is important, and so is sharing the score. Measure what will make a difference, and ensure that appropriate feedback mechanisms exist to provide the score to the people who need it.

» **Consequences**—everyone should know what will happen if expectations are not met. Then follow through when necessary.

Employees, your children, or anyone else within your sphere of influence should expect leader accountability when ensuring clarity in each of these areas. You can be sure you are accountable and performing at the level people need from you by consistently conducting climate surveys.

IT ISN'T GOING TO BE EASY

When you start doing climate surveys and asking about your performance, I guarantee you will hear things you don't want to hear or think about. Here's how one of my clients put it:

> Absolutely every negative comment is a dagger in my heart. There might be a thousand great comments and only one negative, but I guarantee you that I will zero in on that negative and it will hurt a lot. The only reason I'm willing to go through the process is that I know it's the only way to get better and be the leader I want to be.

Your reaction may not be this extreme, but I can assure you that some of the comments you read will be very hard to handle. So you'll probably find it a good idea to review your survey responses when your team members aren't around. Use a weekend or other time away to review the surveys, work through any despair or anger, and move on to the positive steps you intend to take to improve.

THREE COMMITMENTS TO MAKE

Before we get to the details of conducting your first climate survey, you need to make three commitments. If you're unwilling to do these things, you won't get the important benefits you should receive from climate surveys.

1. **Commit to making climate surveys a permanent part of your leadership.** You won't stay clean forever after taking one bath. And you won't keep growing as a leader if you do only one climate survey.
2. **Commit to working to hear the truth in your survey results.** Not everything you read will be fair or friendly, and a lot will make you uncomfortable. It takes real work to find the important truths in your surveys. But if you don't do that, you won't know what to improve.

3. **Commit to sharing the results and working to improve.** Sharing the results and visibly working to improve your performance are a key part of your leadership by example. If you're not willing to work at improving your leadership based on your climate survey results, there isn't much point in doing a survey at all.

CREATING A CLIMATE SURVEY

Servant leaders build character and trust by conducting climate surveys. They ask questions both formally and informally about how they are performing.

I suggest that you do your first climate survey anonymously. That's because the survey should be all about the information, not about who said what.

Make your surveys simple. Here are some questions that have worked for me.

» Am I delivering on my commitments to you?
» Do I provide consistent and respectful feedback to you?
» Am I truthful in my dealings with you?
» Do you feel comfortable telling me disappointing news?
» Am I challenging you to find ways to improve our business?
» Am I staying true to our stated values?
» Have I been an effective coach for you?

Once you ask these questions and you get the feedback, be sure to act on their suggestions. If you don't truly have plans to improve and act on their suggestions, don't ask the questions.

When you have the opportunity to review the information, it's time to share with your direct reports. Here's how I think that session should go.

» **Thank them for the feedback.** Tell them you appreciate it because it will help you be a better leader.
» **Tell them what you think they told you.** There may be a lot to work on, especially in the first few surveys, so you have to

narrow the field to be effective. Explain that you're not sharing everything, just the most important things you will be working on.

» **Tell them what you will be working on.** You may be tempted to work on several things, because they all seem important. Resist that temptation. Research on personal development has consistently shown that we can only work on a limited number of things if we want to be effective. Two or three is about the maximum. If you try to work on more, you will probably discover that you don't make much improvement on anything.

» **Ask for their help in making the change.** This is mutual accountability.

And then, come back to them in two months and ask them if you're doing what you promised. Ask, "Are you seeing that course correction? Are you seeing improvement?"

That's how you build an environment of no fear. You ask the question: "Where can I improve?" You make the improvement. You ask the question again: "Where can I improve?" You make the improvement. When people see you listening to their input about how you can improve, that will send your character skyrocketing in their eyes. You will be setting the example for them to follow.

CLIMATE SURVEYS BRING YOUR SERVANT LEADERSHIP INTO FOCUS

I saved the climate survey chapter for this point in the book, because it's how you make the other parts work. When you want to improve performance as a servant leader, or anything else, you must do three things.

1. **You must try the behavior that you want to learn.** Reading about it alone won't do. You have to act.
2. **You must get feedback.** Without feedback, you'll never learn what needs to improve or whether you're improving.

3. **You must act on the feedback you get to improve your performance.** Then you get more feedback and adjust and get more feedback and adjust… for as long as you're a leader.

EXERCISE

Commit yourself to a climate survey process that will help you understand areas you need to improve. You want to find out what it is like to be on the other side of you!

JESUS IS
MY COACH

THE SECRET

But when he, the Spirit of truth, comes, he will guide you into all the truth. He will not speak on his own; he will speak only what he hears, and he will tell you what is yet to come.

~ John 16:13

Since I started my consulting work at Triune Leadership Services, I have been exposed to some amazing leaders who look to Jesus for guidance within their businesses on a consistent basis. Each of these leaders has the most profound faith, absolutely grounded on Biblical principles, and they're always looking for how to please Jesus within their business and daily activity. They inspire me every day.

Those leaders demonstrate what servant leadership can look like. That doesn't mean that everything is always rosy within their organizations. They have to overcome the same obstacles and meet the same challenges as other leaders. And, often, they make it look easy, like they know some secret that other leaders don't know.

I get asked about that when I conduct Servant Leadership Roundtables or give a speech. People ask for the secret of servant leadership. They want to know the key thing they should do so everything falls into place. They're usually thinking about things we've discussed in this book.

» Is it the foundation? Is defining your purpose, values, and vision the secret?
» How about developing and recognizing people? Is that it?
» Is coaching the secret? It's different from what most managers learned to do.
» Having coaches and mentors is important. Is that the secret?
» What about building relationships? They're critical, after all.
» Is the secret the hard work of seeking and acting on feedback?

Those, and many other things, are important. One of them may even be your blasting cap that sets off a larger explosion of productivity and high morale. But all of those things are techniques. They're part of a system, and they all have to work together if you want to be a successful leader. But they're not *the secret*.

THE SECRET

Whatever happens, great faith-based servant leaders know that they are being propped up each day with the Lord's strength, wisdom, and guidance, and they lead accordingly. The secret is how they call on the Lord for strength, for wisdom, and for guidance. *The secret is prayer.*

I know this from personal experience. My secret, and what I lean on every day—in fact, continually throughout each day—is prayer. Without asking for God's guidance, strength, wisdom, and discernment, I could not begin to be effective in any of these areas. You have to invite Jesus to the party.

Leadership is a tall task, with an extreme amount of responsibility and accountability. I have found that inviting Jesus to help guide your activities as a leader is key to effectively serving others. Thinking about others above and beyond yourself is unnatural for most of us. That's one reason we need God's help and guidance, and why I make prayer a regular part of my life.

Before I get in front of anyone in a training session, I ask for God's guidance to bring the words that will provide the necessary instruction for the completion of His will. Before every coaching session I conduct, I ask God to clear my head of my agenda, and focus on the agenda of the person I am coaching. I ask God to help me to partner and listen at a level that will allow me to help advance his or her agenda in an accelerated fashion.

An awful lot is written about leadership. This morning I searched Amazon for leadership books. There were more than 200,000 of them! And there will be more by the time you read this. What separates faith-based servant leaders from other leaders is that we strive to follow Jesus' example and lead with a servant's heart. The next chapter will go into more detail.

Before you turn the page, though, take a moment to pray for the wisdom to discern the Lord's will, the courage to act, and the strength to persevere.

LEADING THROUGH JESUS' GUIDANCE

I will instruct you and teach you in the
way you should go;
I will counsel you with my loving eye on you.
~ Psalm 32:8

I've already mentioned Vern Anderson and how important he has been in my life. Vern has modeled servant leadership for me and taught me what it means to lead through Jesus' guidance.

Every morning Vern is up early, reading the Bible and praying to learn what God has to say to him for the day. Then he journals those thoughts so he can refer to them throughout that day and in the future.

Because he's a successful businessman and a superb listener, Vern was the perfect coach for me when I was thinking about starting Triune Leadership Services. A lot of things had to happen before I could do that, and I often got anxious, but Vern was always patient with me.

We would pray together and he would calm me down. He would assure me that God would make things clear to me when the time was right. That's how it happened. Vern told me that if I was patient in my prayer and reflection on God's will for my life, things would work out. And they have.

Vern Anderson is a great coach, but there is no better coach than Jesus. He is a phenomenal listener and always guides the best way forward. He is the ultimate model of servant leader that we can all pattern our leadership after. I've seen Jesus' example of servant leadership lived out in the lives of leaders like Vern.

Vern was one of the leaders on a Business Ethics panel I facilitated at a Lunch and Learn session in Alexandria, Minnesota. It was a great experience for me, because I had the opportunity to listen to four amazing leaders talk about living out their faith at work. Here's a quick description of the other panel members.

Tom Schabel is the CEO of Alexandria Industries. He is the consummate servant leader. I have had more people that work within his organization tell me about what an amazing servant leader Tom is, than for any other leader at any company I have ever worked with.

Tim Cullen is the owner of Cullen's Home Center in Alexandria. Tim has been conducting a weekly Bible study at his store for contractors and employees for years.

The fourth panel member was Brent Smith. He's the CEO of the Aagard Group. Brent lives by one of the coolest personal-purpose statements: "Lift people up and make Jesus smile."

The common thread that ran through the discussion was their profound faith in Jesus. All four men clearly lean on God for daily guidance on their decisions and activities. Here are a few of the specific things they do.

» They start every day in prayer with their senior leaders.
» They pray before making any major decision.
» They have a clear set of values they use as a guide for decision-making.
» They work hard to stay focused on the purpose of the organization.

There were many more specifics, but as I listened to these four men talk about how they strive to be Christian leaders in their different companies, I was struck by some common themes.

They all chose to live out their faith every day in every part of their lives. Faith wasn't something they lived on Sunday and put away on Monday. It wasn't something they lived at home, but avoided at work. They were faithful people everywhere and all the time.

All four men demonstrated that you can run a business based on Christian principles and be successful. Servant leadership isn't some soft, fuzzy idea that's at odds with hard-headed business realities. Servant leadership is soft-hearted but tough minded. It's leadership the way Jesus did it. Faith-based servant leaders use Jesus as the model for the way they lead.

JESUS BUILT THE FOUNDATION

Jesus had a clear purpose, values, and vision which culminated on Easter morning. Servant leaders communicate an organization's purpose, values, and vision. They understand that a compelling purpose leads to passion in the workplace. They recognize that they are submissive to their purpose, values, and vision. They are stewards of everything God has given them.

JESUS BUILT ENERGY

Jesus inspired people. He shared His purpose and vision with His disciples, got them engaged in His purpose, and developed their skills. He started with a handful of followers who went on to create a community of faith more than two billion strong. Servant leaders engage their people by clearly communicating their purpose, values, and vision. They let their people know how important their work is in the achievement of the purpose. They set up boundaries for people and put them in control of their goals. Servant leaders are relentless in recognizing people for their work. They are also passionate about providing development opportunities for their people to help them achieve their God-given potential.

JESUS BUILT PERFORMANCE

Jesus challenged people in His day, and He challenges us today. He reminds us that the status quo is not okay and challenges us to keep growing as believers and as leaders. Servant leaders understand it is imperative to be relentless about continuous improvement. Getting comfortable will lead to complacency, which will lead to a decline in an organization's success and effectiveness. So servant leaders set expectations for their team and themselves. They use performance evaluation and coaching to drive continuous improvement.

JESUS BUILT RELATIONSHIPS

Jesus built relationships throughout His life with all people, including some who weren't necessarily the most popular at that time. He demonstrated the patience, kindness, humility, respectfulness, selflessness, forgiveness, honesty, and commitment that servant leaders strive to emulate. Servant leaders understand that building effective relationships will lead to organization success. They treat people with mutual respect and trust, and they lead by listening first.

JESUS BUILT CHARACTER

Jesus was the ultimate model of a servant, coming into a sinful world, to truly take our burdens upon His shoulders and provide a promise of salvation through the sacrifice of His life on the cross. Jesus set the example for His disciples and for us. Servant leaders understand that their actions speak louder than their words. They realize that what they allow in their presence becomes the rule of their command. They are also vulnerable enough to ask and find out how their people feel about their leadership and their declared values, and then make the necessary adjustments to continue to improve their leadership.

CONCLUSION

Thank you for taking the time to read this book. The fact that you did so indicates to me that you are already a highly successful leader with a passion for continued development. I'll be adding new resources to the website to help you, so I hope you'll check there regularly.

You are now on your way to moving from a focus of success to one of significance. Clearly, Jesus' work while on earth was significant. He is calling on each of us to do significant work as well. I am extremely excited for you as you passionately step into being extremely intentional about becoming the servant leader that God created you to be!

Blessings on your journey!

ACKNOWLEDGEMENTS

You can't do servant leadership alone and you can't write a book like this alone. It truly takes a village.

My personal Lord and Savior, Jesus Christ inspired every word that you will read in this book. The scriptures showed me the life He lived and the way He led. His answers to my prayer and reflection gave me insight and inspired me.

He also worked through the people who had a significant positive impact on Leading Jesus' Way. My wife, Kim, actively supported this project for more than two years. She and my younger son, Dan, have spent countless hours reading through the manuscript and giving feedback to make it better. My older son, David, has been a role model for leadership and provided steady support for the book project.

My book writing coach, Wally Bock, gave me all the guidance and direction that someone who had never written a book would need. Leading Jesus' Way would not be the book it is without Wally's guidance, wisdom, and patience with me. I am blessed to count him as a friend and mentor!

My culture coach, Chris Edmonds, helped me understand how to be intentional about building a culture within an organization. He encouraged me to take the time to share my experiences and knowledge by writing this book.

I'm thankful for the many great leaders I had the opportunity to work with over the years. They modeled behavior and shared insights that have become part of me and part of this book.

Vern Anderson, Tom Schabel, Tim Cullen, and Brent Smith are all good friends and role models for how to live your faith at work. They bring servant leadership to life every day. They encouraged me to establish Triune Leadership Services to share with others the impact that leading Jesus' way can have on people, families, organizations, and communities. They had faith in me and I will be forever thankful to them for their encouragement to spread the word on servant leadership.

ABOUT THE AUTHOR

Mark Deterding grew up in Central Illinois in what he calls "the greatest family anyone could ever ask for." His mother was his spiritual mentor and his first servant leadership role model. She was always helping others and always the first one to volunteer when the church needed something done. In his teens, Mark developed the practices of Bible study and prayer that guide his life today.

Mark loved playing sports of all kinds. His father never missed a game when Mark was playing and always found time to help him develop his skills. Mark's father worked in a printing plant as a supervisor. When Mark began working there in his teens, he saw how his father led by serving others. He saw firsthand how high standards and accountability for results can go hand-in-hand with building people up. The way his father led became Mark's model for what good leadership looks like.

After he graduated from college, Mark embarked on a 30-year career in the printing industry where he developed purpose-driven, values-based teams in all aspects of the business. The companies he worked for rewarded his performance with steady promotion, until he was responsible for a staff of ten general managers with indirect responsibility for more than 3000 employees.

He developed the principles he'd learned from his father and his understanding of leadership. In 1993, he completed the University of Minnesota Carlson School of Management's Executive Education program. Gradually his practical experience and study of scripture came together as his understanding grew that Jesus was not only a role model for teachers and preachers, He is also the perfect role model for leaders. Mark began to use the term "servant leadership" to describe the principles he had learned and Jesus had modeled.

When his company was acquired in 2007, Mark faced a challenge. For years, his personal values were aligned with the company where he worked. That wasn't the case with new management. Rather than stay, Mark chose to leave the company where he had worked for over 27 years, and pray for guidance about what to do next.

He went to work for the largest privately held printer in North America for three years, and then decided to pursue his real passion. In 2011 he started Triune Leadership Services to work with leaders and help them develop core servant leadership capabilities that allow them to lead at a higher level and enable them to achieve their God-given potential. Working with organizations, leadership teams, and executives one-on-one, he helps bring focus, clarity, and action to make things work. He also conducts training programs to teach faith-based servant leadership principles.

In 2012 the International Coach Federation designated Mark as an Associate Certified Executive Coach (ACC). He is featured in Ken Blanchard's book *Leading at a Higher Level,* and has been a featured speaker for the Ken Blanchard Companies Executive Forum in both 2007 and 2011. He regularly speaks to organizations and executive forums on the principles of servant leadership and how to make them work.

In addition to his duties at Triune Leadership Services, Mark also serves on the Board of Directors for the Unity Foundation, Mt. Carmel Ministries, and NorthStar Christian Academy all in Alexandria, Minnesota.

Mark and his wife, Kim, live in Alexandria. They have two sons, two lovely daughters-in-law, and three wonderful grandchildren, so far.

ADDITIONAL RESOURCES
FOR *LEADING JESUS' WAY*

*L*eading Jesus' Way is a daily challenge and a never-ending quest. No one book or program will be enough. That's why I've created a collection of "Learning Materials" specifically crafted to help you get the most out of reading and applying, *Leading Jesus' Way*.

Simply visit www.leadingjesusway.com to access your free materials and enter the passcode: servantleadership (case sensitive).

You'll find learning materials to help you get the most out of the book and additional resources including the Forms Packet, my "35 Days of Encouragement" and additional books, websites and more to help you truly integrate *Leading Jesus' Way* into your life.

Blessings on your journey ahead!

Mark

Made in the USA
Columbia, SC
08 November 2022

70667172R00128